This Job Should Be
FUN!

This Job Should Be
FUN!

By Bob Basso, Ph.D.
with Judi Klosek, J.D.

BOB ADAMS, INC.
PUBLISHERS
Holbrook, Massachusetts

Published by Bob Adams, Inc., 260 Center Street, Holbrook Massachusetts, 02343.

ISBN: 1-55850-015-4

Printed in the United States of America.

Cover design by Carole Miguel, Belknap Publishing and Design, Honolulu, Hawaii.

This publication is designed to provide accurate and authoritative information with regard to the subject matter covered. It is sold with the understanding that the publisher is not engaged in rendering legal, accounting, or other professional advice. If legal advice or other expert assistance is required, the services of a competent professional person should be sought.

From a *Declaration of Principles* jointly adopted by a committee of the American Bar Association and a Committee of Publishers and Associations.

To productivity's real heroes--all those who understand that if your work isn't a celebration of your talents, then it is nothing at all.

CONTENTS

Light Manager's Profit Strategies

Appendices

Appendix E
Blank Evaluation Forms/ 247

ACKNOWLEDGMENT

The authors wish to acknowledge the light that never failed--researcher Sharon Minasian and her fabulous traveling magic show. She was somehow able to transform herself into a bulldog, a purring kitten, a piledriver, and, at times, even appear to be in three different places at the same time.

"Labor without joy is base."

John Ruskin
(1819-1900)

Caution!

Exercise extreme caution when presenting this book as a gift to a T.S.S.U.P.A.W. * (pronounced too-super). You know who they are: that vast legion of tragedians who view their job as brain surgery without anesthesia. This book is beneficial to their health, but they are genetically unprepared for its central theme: If you're not managing for fun at work, you're not doing it right. Have some aspirin and water handy, just in case.

*Terminally Serious Sanctimonious Uptight Person at Work

Straight Talk

Bottom line first

Can you have fun on the job and still be productive? After interviewing over 12,000 CEOs, managers, and front line workers, we've found that the answer is a resounding and provable "yes." And that's not all.

Herman Cain, the supercharged, "we-shall-overcome-no-matter-what" CEO of the Godfather Pizza chain, represents the experience of a whole new breed of top guns when he says, "Nobody motivates today's workers. If it doesn't come from within, it doesn't come. Fun helps remove the barriers that allow people to motivate themselves."

These New Breed Workers want to know more and be more. And they want much more than security. They want to use up their lives in tasks that have meaning. They want their sweat to count. If their work is dull and meaningless, then at least they want to be treated like human beings. If they're not, they blow the whistle quickly.

> We don't need better management theories. We need better people managing.

Only managers like Cain--who believe in making work fun, who see through the pursuit-of-excellence syndrome as a hype without heart until you first insure meaning and satisfaction at work--will succeed in our new do-more-with-less economy.

We call these new leaders **Light Managers**.

They hear the shouts of the New Breed Worker and they respond, quickly. They're building super teams in super-tough times by "lightening up" every step of producing quality.

This Job Should Be Fun

They've made fun part of a value system we will constantly refer to in this book:

> # I CARE!
> # YOU MATTER!
> # THIS JOB SHOULD BE FUN!

We've seen this value system work to hasten and reinforce the only edge any business or organization has to break from the pack: *cooperation.*

These Super Teams have moved away from Dinosaur Management--they're talking straight, solidifying the team, sharing power, opening communications, and making *fun* on the job the new standard.

In the long run, all of us--lawyers, nurses, firemen, secretaries, and trapeze artists--feel the simple gut truth: IF OUR LIFE AT WORK IS NOT FUN. IT'S MEANINGLESS. Satisfaction is the only fuel we've got to keep our candle burning.

Light managers know it also fattens the bottom line.

66 Many business people have mourned the death of the work ethic in America. But few of us have applauded the logic of the new value taking its place: 'Work should be fun.' That outrageous assertion is the value that fuels the most productive people and companies in this country. **99**

John Naisbitt
Patricia Aburdene
Re-inventing the Corporation
Warner Books, 1985

This book is about some of those people and companies producing profit and making fun for the workers who do it.

7

Everything You Ever Wanted To Know About FUN at Work But Were Too Serious To Ask

Light Manager's Notebook

Re: The definition of "Productive Fun"--the kind that shows up on the bottom line.

❝ You've got to give people the **freedom** to be innovative; you've got to let them be **responsible** for quality; you've got to let them be **proud** of their work. Then hold them responsible for performance and results--and the work gets to be **fun**. ❞

> Melvin R. Goodes
> President, U.S. Operations
> Warner-Lambert Co.,
> Morris Plain, New Jersey

The Fun Survey that closed the door on Dinosaur Management

In the last eight years we've interviewed or done case studies on 192 CEOs, 2,700 middle managers, and 11,000 workers on the line on the subject of fun.

The findings were overwhelming. Here is the bottom line on fun at work.

1 It means many different things to many different people, but successful companies have more of it.

2 A new, independent, "Don't Tread On Me" worker has emerged, one who has a dominating urge to enjoy his/her job and who sees fun as the logical expression of that joy.

3 The sun has set on Dinosaur (autocratic) Managers. They don't know how to motivate the New Breed Worker.

4 A happy worker produces more. While a very few don't need fun on the job to be happy, the vast majority do.

5 There are a lot of unfunny bosses out there who achieve amazing results by "lightening up" their work environment.

6 The biggest single obstacle to personal productivity is fear.

And many people are scared as hell.

What kind of FUN are we talking about here?

The kind New Breed Worker Judy South, a manager at Taco bell in Tustin, California, talked about when she told us,

> *"When corporate gave us permission to come out from behind the counter and mingle with the customers, we felt more control. Everything got better. Now work is great fun!"*

So this is a book about participative management?

No! This is a book about how to provide the most productive environment for your employees to buy in to participative management by using a Light Manager's approach to productive *fun*.

Wait a minute! What's a Light Manager?

New times, new leaders

Light Manager n. 1. One who causes productivity by sending the message : I Care--You Matter--This Job Should Be Fun. 2. A leader who tells the truth, shares power, listens a lot, superstars the front line, and parks his/her car where everybody else parks theirs.

v.t. 1. To realize that the only way to improve quality is to allow people to enjoy their work, laugh, celebrate, and feel good. 2. To learn the lesson of the great champions of the world . . .

Lighten Up and Win!

13

FUN--with eyes clearly fixed on the bottom line

Light Managers get better results than other managers in tough times. They know the new secret to get people to do more with less. Brad Jencks, GM of Maui Inter-Continental Hotel, Maui, knows it when he dresses up like a chambermaid at a pep rally to announce he's giving everybody the authority to do whatever they think is right to satisfy the guest.

Dick Brooks, CEO of a forty-million-dollar chemical manufacturing business in Massachusetts, knows it when he gives out his home phone number to his front line with the instructions to call him any time they see a glitch in quality. Charles La Rosa had it in mind when he took his key people at American Home Food Products, Inc., from New York to the Arizona desert to have a giant "water fight" so conflicting departments could loosen up and start playing like a team.

Lisa Bergson, CEO of MEECO in Warrington, Pennsylvania, shows it every time she calls a "stress break," takes her team outdoors to play volleyball, and declares, "Absolutely no phone calls during the game." Joel Slutzky of Odetics, a high-tech firm in Anaheim, California, understands it when he declares the "Fun Committee" to be the new corporate culture.

The New Breed Worker . . .

Has a new basic motivation that changes everything we thought we knew about productivity.

> *"I want to enjoy my work."*
> *"I want to participate in the decisions that control my life."*
> *"I want the boss to show me extraordinary care."*

14

Light Managers know that . . .

. . . in tough times . . .

> The more self-determination you allow New Breed Workers, the greater the productivity you get from them.
>
> AND . . .
>
> People work most effectively when they believe it's their idea... not yours.

So celebrate their ideas.

Control + Celebration + Care =

$$\frac{\text{FUN}}{\text{BOTTOM LINE}}$$

Look what Ben did

Ben Strohecker, CEO of Harbor Sweets Chocolate Manufacturing in Salem, Massachusetts, believed his folks were having a ball being in control, so he took *a year off.* When he returned, his team had increased profits by one million dollars. The company was able to pay off most of its debt; the company recorded the best year in its history. All when the boss was away!

Light Managers can do that.

15

This Job Should Be Fun

How do light managers use fun to manage people to produce the results they want--and that the company wants?

Light Managers realize it's impossible to manage people. You can only manage the messages you send them. And LMs always package those messages within the three most basic New Reality Values--the can't-miss messages that tend, more than any others, to encourage people to succeed:

> I Care
> You Matter
> This Job Should Be Fun!

You can only maximize your productivity when you satisfy the basic needs of your team.

The New Breed Attitude: "Why should I give you
                            extraordinary effort to get
                            what you want when you
                            show minimum effort to give
                            me what I need?"

More than eighty-one percent
of the "Fun Survey" respondents said or
indicated this thought as their main
skepticism!

Aren't a few yucks around the water cooler, dressing up at Halloween, and pies in the face at the company picnic all you need to keep things light?

No!

Fun must be a part of the system, a blazing, alive value that continuously feeds the *I Care/You Matter* message. Remember, in the new reductionist economy you're asking people to produce more with fewer resources . . . and win! Only constant reinforcement keeps the spirit of care alive.

Jay Chiat, co-founder of the immensely successful Chiat-Day-Mojo Ad Agency says, "Fun is not something you relegate once a year to planned activities. It has to be part of the environment. It has to be ongoing. It has to be a goal to keep workers happy."

He says that while standing in the belly of giant silver whale he constructed for his team's conference room.

Light Manager's notebook

Re: How fun really produces: It jiggles the toilet!
(A note from coauthor Bob Basso.)

"I was sitting in seat 12C of a Boeing 737, checking my speech notes for my keynote address to the American Dental Association in Chicago.

"About an hour out of O'Hare Airport, the tail section started to shake like a barn door in a Kansas duster. We all played the 'I'll-act-like-it's-not-really-happening' game and tried not to look back.

"The shaking got worse, and, when the flight engineer ran down the aisle banging his flashlight, angrily exclaiming in a loud, clear voice, 'These damn things never work in an emergency,' the passengers in the back rushed forward to empty seats. We all put on our Nearer-My-God-To-Thee faces and got real quiet.

"A large man with one of those two-foot-square cowboy belt buckles got up against the stewardess' protestations and went to the john. He came out with a big smile on his face and boomed, 'Don't worry, folks. It's just the damn toilet. I jiggled the handle. Everything's gonna be fine now.'

"Instant relief. Everybody laughed and kept on laughing.

"Then (and may I never receive another royalty dollar from another book if the following is not the unfettered truth) in less than two minutes the mysterious shaking stopped. The place went wild with laughter.

"Everything was fine until our approach to O'Hare. The death rattle began anew. Instantly the pilot got on the intercom and calmly intoned, 'Would the gentleman who jiggled the toilet handle before give it another shot.'

"More laughter, and Flight 182 landed safely in the misty night. Later we learned that the pilot had shut down one engine and had only half power in another, a very serious situation, but we didn't mind a bit. We were too busy laughing and acting like we knew we were going to make it all along."

The Bottom Line

> Fun and humor change people's perception of pain. They don't stop the "shaking" but they minimize fear and let you land the plane safely. They allow you to face monsters and still be in control. At work today we are facing the biggest monsters we've ever faced. They have spine-tingling names like "restructuring," "downsizing," "merger," "leveraged buy-out," "restraint," "pay freeze," "foreign competition," and, worst of all, "a no-nonsense CEO."

Lighten up!

Light Manager's notebook

Re: How important is fun as a motivator?

"How many friends--and how much **fun**--we have is the key to happy living."

> Findings, USA Today
> Life Quality Index

"I'm drained. It's no **fun** any more."

> Barry Switzer
> Former Oklahoma football coach
> (resignation statement)

"Most people look at work as a necessary drag. I don't. I think it's great **fun**."

> Ralph Nader
> Consumer Advocate

"I'd rather work in my garden than keep my job. I guess the bottom line is that it's not **fun** any more."

> Barbara Stanwyck, actress
> (upon quitting her popular TV series,
> "The Colbys")

"I decided to change things, to loosen up our practices. I did and suddenly we began having **fun** again. And we also began winning."

> Pat Riley
> former coach, L.A. Lakers

20

C'mon. How does fun affect the bottom line?

It simplifies, clarifies, and unifies effort toward a common goal. How?

Productive fun . . .

Creates an environment of acceptance

Raises the expectation that things are going to get better

Cements cooperative effort (like nothing else)

Productive FUN creates an environment of acceptance

In 1981, computers had been around a while--but half the consumers were downright intimidated over anything so small being so much smarter than the operator, and the other half were afraid they'd never learn how to turn one on. IBM knew that when they unveiled the PC (Personal Computer). That's why they chose a universal symbol of fun to soften the image of their revolution in a box--Charlie Chaplin.

Charlie helped the world forget its fear and intimidation just by being there. The PC went from zero to five billion dollars in sales in three years and captured eighty percent of the world market.

21

Productive FUN raises expectations

People reach the level of expectation you set for them. Usually, all a good manager has to do is announce that expectation and keep repeating, "I know you can do it" to meet the goal. Lee Iacocca kept telling Chrysler workers he expected them to take charge of quality and improve it, and they did. President Kennedy pounded away on the theme of volunteering to make a better America ("Ask not what your country can do for you . . ."), and citizens responded in record numbers. But . . . *if you clothe the expectation in fun, you get there quicker.*

Look at what Taco Bell did to improve customer service.

> ## Watch what happens the next time you order that scrumptious Burrito Supreme!

In 1988, Taco Bell President John Martin decided to shift the focus of his 49,700 employees from operations to interacting with the customers. As he put it, "We wanted to make it more fun for everybody to come from behind their out-of-sight work areas and meet the customers who use the product and pay the bills."

He reduced the size of the kitchen and installed machinery that allowed the cooks to work less and come out and mingle with the customers.

Employees like Judy South, manager of one of his outlets, love it: "It's not hard work any more. We look forward to coming to work. It's fun."

Taco Bell's profits increased thirty-eight percent that year.

Productive FUN cements cooperative effort (like nothing else)

Only cooperative effort makes winners in losing times. Managers have got to break down obstacles to clear communication, erase petty bickering, and get everybody pulling on the same rope.

> Every winning team we studied had major differences within the ranks, but they had all instituted fun programs that allowed everybody to cross over into one another's territory and get the job done.

Winning Teams have a remarkable ability to equalize everybody and solidify the team with planned fun.

Browning Management Company in Carmel, Indiana, declares every other Friday "Casual Day," when folks can wear any kind of fun clothing they want. Teamwork is noticeably more efficient and productivity shoots up twenty-five percent on that day. KTOO-TV in Juneau, Alaska, breaks out the champagne and cookies and celebrates all victories, from painting the office to new births to success in the ratings. Every department is invited. They are consistently rated an excellent station. Apple Computer is recognized for having one of the most innovative and enthusiastic teams in the world of high tech. Their glue: a constant array of team fun, including Friday afternoon beer busts and a tradition of allowing many of their folks to write their own job descriptions and give themselves whatever title they deem appropriate.

23

Can you be a light manager if you're not a funny person?

Absolutely.

There is a distinction between "funny" and "lightening up."

According to our survey, most managers of winning teams didn't pose a threat to Henny Youngman or Joan Rivers, but they knew how to give permission to their teams to make worker involvement a lighthearted journey.

How do they do it? Read the rest of this book.

We've taken the best practical "lighten up" programs with a proven track record for the bottom line results and outlined how to do them in simple steps.

"Okay, okay. I understand FUN and a lighthearted environment make you feel good and momentarily relieve the pain in your molars from biting the bullet, but . . . ."

> What do you do if you're working for a Terminally Serious Sanctimonious Uptight Person at Work (T.S.S.U.P.A.W)?
> How can you use the Light Manager's techniques?

Well, you can wait until he or she dies, or you can shine on the corner where you are. Start the Revolution without that person. Don't try to change him or her. Change you. It's your life. You have a right to enjoy where you're going to spend forty-one percent of it--at work.

If you're not having fun, you're not doing it right. Lighten up and enjoy! (And wipe that sourpuss expression off your face in tough times...)

Super Teams have super fun in super-tough times

This overwhelming reality became self-evident early on as we investigated the part fun plays in building a healthier bottom line in scary times. The reason is simple:

> *"Fun forges cooperation quicker than any other human dynamic (other than catastrophe). And business today will live or die on how much team effort they can pump into every single production step they take."*

> Henry Donaghy, CEO
> Donaghy Financial Services
> North Carolina

It all starts with sending the message:

> ## I CARE
> ## YOU MATTER
> ## THIS JOB SHOULD BE FUN

General Motors' Rochester Products Division asks its employees for advice on who should be promoted to supervisor. Godfather Pizza writes fun into its mission statement. Xerox Corporation, 3M, and Honeywell help finance start-ups by their teams when the teams present an idea that might fly. Ben and Jerry's Homemade Ice Cream has a Joy Committee. John Smith of Sports 'A Foot hires only positive people, and Brad Jencks, the General Manager of the Maui Inter-Continental Hotel, put on a dress to solve the darkest problem his team faces. Light Managers are making team involvement profitable fun.

A little quiz

Question:	At what period in our nation's work history did we produce more positive literature, songs, films, team cohesion, neighborhood strength, and classic radio comedy?
Answer:	Right. World War II, humanity's darkest hour.

We faced horrifying monsters with fun, laughter, irreverent satire, and a volcanic energy for teamwork and enthusiasm that lifted this planet from the grasp of unspeakable evil and tilted it back toward the sun.

We were all Light Managers then.

We did it before. We can do it again. But not with serious, sanctimonious, uptight starched collars commanding our units. Not with pasty-faced "leaders" from the Darth Vader School of Management who believe work is our punishment for not marrying rich.

Lighten up!

The Light Manager's ACTION check-off

☐ 1. Change your thinking.

The world has changed. Workers want more control over the decisions that affect their lives. Your job is to give it to them. Your productivity, your personal success, and your mental health depend on how well you adapt to satisfy those needs.

☐ 2. If you can't accept the principle above, you're rejecting reality, and that's always unwise.

Take time off, go for a hot air balloon ride, watch some kids playing in the park, smell a few flowers along the way. Then see if resisting Rule #1 makes any sense.

In the New Reality, Light Managers know...

This job has to be fun (control, celebration, care) because that fun puts the New Breed Workers in their highest zone of achievement in tough times.

1

COMMUNICATIONS:
Walk Your Talk

Light Manager's
Profit Strategy #1

I care/ **You matter**	We hide nothing. We respect your ability to handle the truth.
This job should be fun	Give everybody a whistle.

Light Managers know . . .

“ A manager's personal style--how good he or she is at exchanging information--contributes more to a department's efficiency than the results of any structured or organizational brilliance. **”**

Mark H. McCormack, Author,
*What They Don't Teach You
At Harvard Business School*
Bantam Books

Because the line feels . . .

“ Why the hell should we bust our ass for a bunch of shirts and ties [managers] who never tell us what the hell is going on. They act like we're the enemy. Screw 'em. **”**

J.D.,
Shift Foreman
Major New York Garment Factory
(from authors' line survey
of 11,000 workers)

Stop pussyfooting. Walk your talk! Tell the truth!

Super Teams have only one communications policy in tough times: Declare honesty from day one. "I tell you what's going on. You tell me. When one of us breaks that trust, that person walks."

That's pretty tough medicine for most Dinosaur Managers to swallow. Most of them will accept that thought as well as they do sitting for a root canal.

> If you can't tell your team the truth all the time, stop the fraud of teambuilding training.

You can't ask people to continue to sacrifice and do more with less if they can't see what the payoff is for them.

Lay it on the line for your team. Mean what you say. It's the only way to build trust.

Light Manager Mike Weaver, CEO of Weaver Popcorn in Van Buren, Indiana,is a fanatic about truth. He shows all new hires a video tape of the company's last open forum where every employee revels in Weaver's only communication policy: "Talk out and talk back for what you know is right." He tells the rookies to stand up to everybody, including him, when "You know you're right about your work."

Remember: The New Breed Worker wants two crucial questions answered truthfully and often

"How Am I Doing?"

"Where Are We Going?"

How to: After you tell your opening joke, preface every meeting, every conference, every connection, every interaction where two or more are gathered, including the T.G.I.F. beer bust, by answering those two questions, whether they're asked or not.

Don't wait for your annual State of the State Speech. Then it's too late. People are involved in a daily battle with insecurity.

They want to know now!

It all starts with open communications

In a society that has weathered the fatal lies of Watergate, Irangate, sleazy inside trading on Wall Street, million-dollar-a-year S&L presidents getting fatter by defrauding their depositors, and the nearly monthly disgrace of high government officials being reprimanded for heinous ethical and moral crimes--in this environment, corporations that lie, evade, withhold or simply "bottleneck" information are aiding and abetting the rampant fear and distrust of authority.

A team fearful--a team distrustful--will never buy into your goals.

Empower a team by communicating trust

You communicate trust by giving them all the information they want all the time they want it.

Open the floodgates. Let there be a free flow of information up and down the line. And when anybody in your organization can walk up to anybody else and get a straight answer, then you have open communications.

Dinosaurs will resist this openness. They fear a loss of power because they equate withholding information with maintaining control over the line.

Explain to them that an open society that has passed the Freedom of Information Act (1976) allowing citizens access to all the government information that concerns their safety and welfare doesn't tolerate corporations that don't.

If that doesn't work, drop this tidbit in their ear . . .

Case study: Quality and communications

Re: When everybody tells the truth, your business improves. But you may lose a few *zzzzz's*.

Dick Brooks is the founder and CEO of a forty-million chemical manufacturing training business, ChemDesign Corporation, with its headquarters in Fitchburg, Massachusetts.

Brooks, like every chemical producer, is under heavy pressure from the Environmental Protection Agency to cut emissions and get "squeaky clean."

He's gone all out to do just that and more. ChemDesign is shooting for zero emission.

Brooks knows he himself can't reduce pollutants by tiny parts per million. Only his team at the controls can do that, so he's given them his home phone number and told them to call when they feel something isn't right.

They do, and the boss responds.

"I got one call from a fella at our plant in Wisconsin one night," Dick remembers. "He said they had a serious problem. I got on a plane immediately and flew there." As it turned out, it wasn't that serious, but Dick didn't mind a bit.

He understands that when your team feels they can call the number-one boss with a quality problem any time of the day or night, you've got open communications and truth working for your profit picture.

The Bottom Line:

> Productivity units at ChemDesign have increased dramatically, and absenteeism is down to one percent, well below the national average.

"Whistleblowing" is the most cost-effective program you have

Encouraging your team to "blow the whistle" internally when they feel something is wrong is your highest form of quality control. Listening to their suggestions is the most cost-effective program you have.

Consider the billions of dollars spent when GM had to recall the Chevrolet Corvair, whose safety problems were made public by Ralph Nader. (Ford had a similar case with its Ford Pinto, whose exploding gas tanks resulted in several deaths and countless lawsuits.)

Could the tragedy of the January 28, 1986, explosion of the Challenger space shuttle been avoided? Could the lives of seven astronauts have been saved? Could irreparable damage to the future of space exploration and the morale of NASA employees have been averted?

Engineers at the company that made the defective rockets which caused the disaster said they had told their managers of the problem but their managers chose to ignore their concerns.

Tell your Dinosaurs this--and tell them:

Erase the "Us" vs. "Them" relationship!

Once you require your team to be loyal to the truth first and the company second, you establish the strongest concept possible in team building--"we"--and that makes everybody more powerful.

The free flow of information removes fear and puts everybody on the same side

Pitney Bowes demonstrates their "open door" policy by supporting their shareholders meeting with a job holders meeting, where groups of two or three hundred workers can ask management any question they want.

Those who submit the best question are awarded a fifty-dollar savings bond!

Pitney Bowes not only encourages open communications-- they reward it!

> **WE** want you to "blow the whistle" so **WE** can fix it.

Hide nothing. Be obsessive about face-to-face contact in getting the word out all the time.

When your team knows you'll listen and act when they "blow the whistle" inside, there's no need to go outside and call the newspapers, a lawyer, and "60 Minutes."

Make the CEO the chief whistle-blower

All management starts at the top. Your team takes its action cues not from what you say or write in your mission statement, but from what you do. They'll follow your lead if they can see it.

> *"If CEOs wish to create a moral corporate culture, their actions are more persuasive than statements of intent; fair treatment of whistle-blowers may be the most dramatic way to persuade employees to operate ethically."*

Janet P. Near
Associate Professor of Business Administration
Indiana University Graduate School of Business

We'd go a step further and suggest the boss model the behavior, loudly and often.

If you want the people on your team to be fanatics about improving quality, you've got to allow them to *be wrong without fear* and *criticize openly*.

Mike Weaver walks his talk. Every time he makes a mistake that involves the team, he calls them together and uses the words he encourages everybody to use when things go wrong: *"I goofed!"* Then he tells them why and how he fouled up. Result: everybody at Weaver Popcorn speaks their mind openly about improving things. They've also increased profitability fifty percent since they started this program three years ago.

Recently, Weaver's team goofed on 265 shipments to customers. They told Mike. He sat down and wrote every customer, explaining why they goofed, how they did it, and what they were going to do in the future to repair it. Customers were flabbergasted with this honesty, and not one withdrew business.

Light Manager's notebook

Re: To get trust, you've got to give truth.

"Old Blood and Guts" knew.

Many will debate the merits of his personality traits, but no one can deny General George S. Patton, Jr., built one of the greatest super teams, the Third Army, in super-tough times.

Porter B. Williamson, an officer on the staff of "the man the Germans most hated to fight," in his intriguing book on the legendary warrior, writes that Patton did it by using the truth. "With Patton's ability to get the truth to the troops, he had the trust of every soldier. He spoke truth with such a forceful attitude whether it was pleasant information or not. His constant command to the staff was, 'Get the facts, get the truth and get it to the troops.' " Porter adds: "He always delivered the scoop, good or bad, with as much humor as he could."

Patton's team never lost.

This job should be fun

Actually give everybody a whistle

Physicalize the symbol that means the most to your team. Don't bury it in a policy manual. No one reads those things anyway. The whistle says, we really want you to be in charge around here. When you need to know something, blow it and we'll get you the answer. And blow it every time you see something that doesn't match your idea of quality.

Give one to every new hire. Give one to every manager. If you're the CEO, wear one around your neck every time you walk around the front lines. Silly? Not if you mean it.

Muffins with Mr. McBig

There's only one way to "open communications" in an organization--make it easy for everybody to talk to the boss. You make him or her accessible by making it informal fun to chat. Remember, most of your folks would rather lambada with their in-laws than talk to the "the Prez." Set a half-hour in the morning in the employee dining room for anybody to dunk donuts with the CEO and get some straight talk. Change the name of the program according to the Mr./Ms. McBig's name, i.e.: Bagels with Benson; Croissants with Carnosky; Prune Danish with Peters, etc. Watch its impact on every other area of communications.

Electronic reader board

Our lives are driven by instant communications, twenty-four-hour TV news, beepers, mobile phones, fax machines, data bases that punch up the world in milliseconds, and pizza in thirty minutes or less. (An outfit in New England is experimenting with a truck and mobile oven unit that delivers in twelve minutes or less. What's next--edible fax pizza?)

We're used to immediate access to all the information that satisfies our widening "need to know." Why should it be any different at work?

Get one of those electronic reader boards you see at the bank that updates you on news, scores, and the intimate lives of steamy soap opera vixens and put it in the employee dining room.

This Job Should Be Fun

No newsletter, PR release, or hastily called "employee info-sharing meeting" can compare with the instant effectiveness of this method. It's cheap, too. Tell the truth and make it fun with features like "Straight Skinny from Mr./Ms. McBig," "Rumor of the Day," etc. Don't get carried away with the coq au vin recipes and hygiene tips for teenagers. Just put out "the word."

> ## "Burn, baby, burn!"

Prove you really mean to have an "open door" policy. Call a surprise meeting of your entire work team in the parking lot. Announce the new open communications--and then burn every office door in a giant barn fire.

Make certain you alert the fire department and your insurance company. Your team will get the point and hold it for a very long time.

The Light Manager's ACTION check-off

√

1. Call your team together.

Announce your value system. Declare honesty: "Tell the truth or walk."

2. Constanly update.

Hold five-minute "morning quarters" before work begins.

3. Walk your talk.

Keep your word. Answer all questions honestly. Don't "protect" the image of the company. Be honest. If you don't know the answer, say so--and then say, "But I'll find out and give you an answer at (give an exact time and keep it)."

4. Give 'em the power.

Give everyone the power to pull the plug when quality is in doubt.

5. Encourage whistle-blowing.

Provide a hotline for it.

6. Thank the whistle-blower.

Publicly!

7. Open up channels.

Let your people go directly to your boss's boss or higher, if need be, to resolve questions of honesty.

In the New Reality, Light Managers know . . .

Keeping an open atmosphere with a free flow of information up and down is the least expensive and most efficient source of feedback about goofs the organization may be making. Honesty is the best systems management. It immediately clarifies relationships. Most morale problems arise because managers are afraid to recognize and share the truth.

2
FEEDBACK:
Form M-I-B Teams

Light Manager's
Profit Strategy #2

I care/ You matter	You're the experts. Take charge of quality improvement. Management will become fanatics about supporting you.
This job should be fun	"M-I-B (Make-It-Better) Teams" is the biggest game we play around here.

&&You've got to let your team change everything. Make it faster, better, safer, and more fun to be there. If not, you're a 'goodbye business' in a new world that doesn't give a damn about being second-best. **99**

Danielle Cormier
Quality Control Expert
Montpelier, Vermont

Three little words say it all

M-I-B stands for the three most important words in the New Economy:

> ## MAKE IT BETTER
> ### (and deliver it faster)

Super Teams know it's not enough to "hold your own" anymore. The speed of the production merry-go-round is being controlled by hungry foreign competitors who worship at the altar of the gods *faster, better,* and *cheaper.*

Today's consumers are used to instant gratification. They *expect* pizza to be delivered in thirty minutes or less; eyeglasses to be made while they wait; packages to be delivered overnight; the burger with the works to be ready in less than a minute.

If you can't satisfy them, there's somebody down the block who can.

> *Super teams are retooling to speed up both quality and delivery in a supersonic time frame.*

THE LIMITED CLOTHING CHAIN rushes new fashions off the design table and into its 3200 stores in less than 60 days, while most of their competitors still order Christmas apparel the previous May. TOYOTA and HONDA can take a car from concept to market in three years--a breathtaking pace! FORD and GM are closer to five, but are aiming to do it in one. McGRAW-HILL, the publishing giant, can now print and deliver some books within forty-eight hours. Soon, students will be reading history about the same time it happens.

Patriot vs. Scud: The M-I-B story that won far more than just dollars

Raytheon, the $9 billion defense firm that built the stunningly effective Patriot missile system, became a Super Team long before the Persian Gulf conflict. A caring environment was created for the firm's 76,000 employees long before the 1980 Patriot contract. The emphasis: Get involved and make work better at all levels.

The Raytheon culture insisted that management stop and listen to every employee suggestion. "Dedicated Teams" were formed to facilitate employee input, and an "Act Now" program was instituted to cut costs immediately. In addition, Raytheon employees enjoyed constant recognition and informal "Total Quality Time" coffee klatsches with management. The goal of all this was simple: Make It Better!

With that attitude--and with a commitment to open, honest communications--Raytheon proved that American business can shoot down any obstacle to progress . . . as long as the employees share total dedication to defined goals.

> ## Make M-I-B your team's marching orders!

Case study: Let go!

True, Ben Strohecker, president and founder of Harbor Sweets--a top-of-the-line chocolate manufacturer--hires mostly part-time workers. It's also true he allows them incredible flexibility when it comes to scheduling their work. The company's stated policy is that if you want unpaid time off to see Junior play in the Little League game or to stay at home with a sick mother-in-law, take it. But it's also true that this gentle Ben from Salem, Massachusetts, who offers very little more than the minimum wage, offers his team a great deal more of the twin ingredients the New Breed worker craves: trust and respect.

There are no time clocks to punch. All employees are responsible for quality control, and their decision to reject a product line is never questioned. There's no assembly line; workers are grouped into teams, with everybody familiar with everybody else's job, and managers get a simplified profit and loss statement every month. The CEO is very often found on the line, hand-preparing his famous assortment of sweets and smilingly announcing the company philosophy" "If you're not having fun, you're fired."

Why would more than a hundred people give up higher wages in another job to produce, sort, and ship chocolates in the dead of a New England winter? (This is a seasonal business.) Ruth Keyes, aged seventy-one, a ten-year Harbor Sweets veteran, says she finds it a warm and fun workplace.

True, this simple tale of a candy-maker who keeps relinquishing control and authority to his front line doesn't conclusively prove that sending the I CARE--YOU MATTER--THIS JOB SHOULD BE FUN message is the most effective way to manage the New Breed Worker.

Not at all. It just shows how one small-town boss went from a start-up business in his basement to a two-million-dollar operation by putting extraordinary care before profit.

The Bottom Line:

> Extraordinary employee
> commitment to producing the
> highest-quality chocolate possible.

Still . . .

However effective this strategy of quality delivered with quick response . . .

> *Management will not be the one to improve the cycle one millisecond. Only the Team on the line can Make It Better.*

Form M-I-B Teams. They represent a Needback, not Feedback system, one that's really very selfish.

Make-It-Better Teams satisfy *your* need to get the team to buy in to improving everything and *their* need to take more control of the decisions that affect their day-to-day work life.

Thomas Jefferson was the father of M-I-B teams

> *"People, like nations, are motivated by self-interest."*
> T.J.

The key to all motivation is to find out what personal needs people have and satisfy them first before you get them to do what you want.

M-I-B Teams

Background

Definition: A simple, totally democratic *Employee Needback System* comprising small units within a large department or division.

Purpose: To empower a staff to participate with management, guide the organization to higher productivity and increased job fulfillment, and nurture a passion for quality performance at all levels of operation.

Philosophy: People work most effectively when they believe it's their idea. M-I-B Teams offer the worker a maximum opportunity to express his or her solutions and to actively suggest, plan, and implement reform. *M-I-B appeals to the basic and immediate need of the individual to "Make It Better for me."*

How is it different from other participative modes? It is simple, informal, and *open to every member of the department/division.* Suggestions are forwarded and responded to by management *within forty-eight hours.*

M-I-B is not a debating society.
Bring solutions--not problems!

FEEDBACK: Form M-I-B Teams

How does M-I-B work?

When: Once a month (or as many times as the staff feels is necessary.

Where: A quiet, informal space. (Many M-I-B Teams meet for lunch in the park, on the front lawn, etc.)

Length: Forty-five minutes only! (The discipline of a time limit is critical to the success of M-I-B. "We're here to concentrate on the solutions, get to the point, and move on.)

Agenda: Always the same . . . "How can we make it better for all of us?" Address these six categories:

1. Open Communications--How can we keep everybody here more fully informed--and how can we make it easier for people to talk with the people they need to talk with?

2. Improving Quality of Customer Service--How can we better serve the present and future needs of our market--and how can we increase our responsiveness?

3. Cost Savings--How can we simplify the work we do and reduce waste? How can we make everyone more aware of cutting costs?

4. Staff Morale--What can we do to foster more cooperation between departments and individuals? What matters do the staff want handled immediately?

5. Physical Environment--What's wrong with the physical plant that most affects the health and welfare of the staff? How can we better utilize our space?

6. New Ideas (products, services, making work fun)--Let's create new ways of doing things. Keep looking to change everything. How can we put more color and joy into our routines?

This Job Should Be Fun

How M-I-B teams made it better for everybody

Mike Jarrett is the commissioner of a SUPER TEAM of 12,000 employees of the South Carolina Board of Health. They inaugurated their participative management plan with M-I-B two years ago. Mike reports that the teams have

* improved overall communications
* caused idea sharing all around
* made major environmental changes
* reorganized their work patterns

They've made a more efficient, open, team-oriented operation that keeps on winning.

They've also proven that M-I-B is not a "me first, the heck with everybody else" process.

The commissioner who cares about his people was recently diagnosed as having a life-threatening disease. He would undergo treatment that would rob his body of vital blood platelets. His M-I-B Team members immediately initiated a program of massive blood donations to replenish the supply both for Mike and for other people suffering from the same illness.

When you show extraordinary care to your team, you receive it back tenfold. Good luck, Mike.

"What's in it for me?"

* M-I-B puts quality control in the hands of the people most responsible for it.

* Quick response. "Okay, Mr./Ms. Manager. You want me to respond quickly to the needs of our customer. Fine. Show me that behavior. Respond quickly to my needs."

* The title "Make It Better" is the most direct explanation of what everybody around here has to do to win.

You build a SUPER TEAM by showing EXTRAORDINARY CARE to the needs of individuals. The most dramatic way to show EXTRAORDINARY CARE is QUICK RESPONSE.

You'll live and die on your managers' commitments to QUICK RESPONSE.

The key to any feedback system is not to make your employees fanatics about improving *their* jobs. The people on your line are already fanatical about doing their work better. Oh, sure--some may have given up along the way, but probably because somebody "upstairs" doesn't care about them.

> *Make your **managers** fanatics about supporting the front line!*

How do you do that?

If you haven't hired light managers to begin with, then there's only one choice: get tough! Don't tolerate managers who don't respond within forty-eight hours. Once one breaks that cycle, you start sending the most damaging message management can send the New Breed Worker: "I really don't care."

Remember, forty-eight-hour Quick Response doesn't mean you'll have to say "Yes" to all requests. It means you're a fanatic about answering quickly. Most of the time you'll have to say "No." The key is to do it positively.

Reality check: You are bound to have a few dinosaur managers and some Terminally Serious Sanctimonious Uptight Etcetera who see M-I-B as a threat. They fear they'll lose power by allowing the line to participate in major quality decisions.

Target them before the program begins. Let them know the new law of the land. Say, "I need your help." Use positive fear as a motivator: "I expect your M-I-B Team to be a model for the entire operations. Good luck. I'll be watching you closely."

"We're too small for all this stuff. What do we do?"

The "Two-Minute Drill."

Why is it that, during the last two minutes of seemingly every football game, teams go into their "two-minute drill" and run, pass, and kick better than they did in the previous fifty-eight minutes?

Because they have to. Everything is urgent now. People have to concentrate on doing what they do best in order to score points and win.

Do the same thing, but keep M-I-B as the theme. Call "Time out! Two-minute drill!" Gather a few folks around and say, "How can we make it better on the _____?" Ask for answers, not Labor Day speechmaking. Get consensus. *End the game at two minutes.*

It's fast. It's fun. It's the fast-food approach to problem-solving, but that's the way things get done today.

Bottoming out on M-I-B

One Chicago-based publishing house decided to make the phrase "Make It Better!" the battle cry for all their efforts. They used it in speeches, posters, newsletters, bowling shirts, memo pads, on the side of the executive jet, and on their toilet tissue. They removed it from the toilet tissue when an M-I-B Team proved it was a chemical hazard that posed, in their words, "a clear and imminent danger to our bottom line."

What one Light Manager had to do to get his M-I-B point across (a true story)

Murray G., the CEO of a sixty-million-dollar electronic supply business in the midwest, inaugurated M-I-B with almost complete success. Every department showed immediate positive changes in morale and quality of work. All but one--Marketing. The manager there responded late if he responded at all to M-I-B requests.

Murray called in the "old liner" and held up a long, sharp cactus needle.

"Dave, have you ever had one of these stuck in your butt?"

Dave smiled and shook his head, "No."

"Well, believe me, it hurts. Two are unbearable. More than that and you just have to stop walking near cactus. Either that or cut it down. Every time you refuse to respond to your team, you stick me in the butt."

The boss paused and then handed Dave the needle. Then he smiled and said, "That's one."

The Bottom Line:

Dave eventually got the point. His team went from zero to forty-seven major quality improvements, at a cost savings of over $120,000.

Motivating speeches, training, and pep rallies are nice, but your team learns by example. If you want quick response, you've got to give quick response.

This job should be FUN

Name your team

An electric company in Colorado has M-I-B teams with colorful names:

> "Redhot Mamas and Papas"
> "Flaming Amps"
> "Can-Do Rangers"
> "Static Warriors"
> "Cost Busters"

Fun fuels creativity and keeps the environment loose.

Color your report forms

A smiling face, a cartoon, or a funny saying keeps everybody focused on the "team concept" of M-I-B. Teams that have fun together usually win more games.

Take the show on the road

Encourage breaking the monotony of same meeting, same place. Hold it on the front lawn or brown-bag it at a nearby park.

Yearly themes

Some organizations print a yearly theme across all the M-I-B forms. Some examples:

> "Cooperation Gets Us All What We Want."
> "Cut Costs, Win Big Bucks" (Incentive Program)
> "Every Team Member a Quality Control Expert"
> "Change Everything--Make It Work Better"

To be most effective, themes should be chosen by the employees.

Yearly awards party

A dinner/dance party thrown by management for everyone who participated in M-I-B teams, with awards for outstanding achievements in:

Number of suggestions * Number of suggestions implemented * Number of cost-saving suggestions implemented * Number of customer service improvements made * Quickest response time manager * CEO Trophy (or cash reward) for M-I-B Team that did the most to further the good image of the company or organization * The Spirit Award--to the M-I-B team member who most exemplifies the spirit of cooperation and team play.

The Light Manager's ACTION check-off

✔

☐ **1. Call your department together.**

Explain the M-I-B Team concept. Sell it. (See the Appendices section of this book for more ideas.) Get four to seven employees to commit to holding the first meeting. Schedule it. Hold it.

☐ **2. Get a facilitator.**

Get a facilitator from the training department to sit in. You stay away. It's their meeting, not yours. When they want you there, they'll invite you.

☐ **3. Don't get bogged down with rules.**

Stay simple and flexible. Let your people develop their own approach to M-I-B. Give them assistance only when they ask for it, and then refer them to another M-I-B Team that seems to be doing well. Let them learn from one another.

☐ **4. Be positive.**

Respond within forty-eight hours. Be positive, even when you have to say "no." Keep using the phrase "Make It Better" in all your approaches to improvement.

In the New Reality, Light Managers know . . .

The most effective way to work is to give your team the freedom to do it their way.

Constantly send the message, "The person you work for is no longer responsible for your work. You are. Not me, not your supervisor, not the CEO--*you!*"

"*You* have to make it better for *you*. I'll help."

3

USE A BATTLE CRY:
Create Excitement
Start a Raging Fire

Light Manager's
Profit Strategy #3

I care/ You matter	"You deserve a clearly definable goal that, when reached, makes you an obvious winner."
This job should be fun	Offer previews of coming attractions.

The right battle cry, constantly reinforced,
will become reality

"We deliver in thirty minutes or less or the pizza is on us."
"Quality is Job 1."
"Think."
"We try harder."

Find the battle cry that creates passionate commitment

Super Teams have one giant neon sign blinking all the time--*We know where we're supposed to be going, and we know what we have to do to get there.*

That sign is constantly reinforced by billboards, banners, advertisements, pep rallies, patches, halftime locker-room speeches, skywriting, parades, and lots of shouting. The Terminally Serious Sanctimonious Etcetera smirkingly refer to all this as a "dog and pony show."

Let them.

> ## Bring on the dog and pony show. It works.

In the modern world of work, filled with the strongest combination of negative emotions we have ever faced, a Battle Cry that awakens positive feelings and breathes life into a goal does more for team self-esteem than all the inspiring speakers who ever pounded a podium.

The key is to find one that creates passion for the behavior that gets you what you want.

In 1962, Avis and every other car rental business was being pounded into a smaller market share by the #1 giant, Hertz. They chose a battle cry that told the truth about their team's effort to be the best. They doubled revenue in three years--and kept the team fired up to this day.

"WE TRY HARDER"

Light Manager's notebook

Re: Why do managers have to create excitement?

Because:

I AM A NEW BREED WORKER.

I am a child of the MTV/Fast-Food Generation.

I have a lightning-short attention span.

I want it slick, quick, and with plenty of pizzazz.

IF YOU DON'T EXCITE ME RIGHT AWAY, you've lost me. I don't read mission statements. I don't give a damn about them if they're not in my language. You want me to ''buy in'' to your goals--then pump me up, excite me with something new, and keep on pumping.

IF YOU BORE ME, I CAN DESTROY YOU by doing just enough to get by--and no more.

How to pick your battle cry

Don't!

Let your team pick it. You coach. Remember, New Breed Workers want control, and will only buy in if they participate in the decisions that affect their work life.

John Smith, the energetic president and founder of the Florida-based Sports'A Foot clothing chain, first asked his team what would make them winners. They shouted back, "We want to have more fun with the customers!"

Their battle cry has been the same for the last four years, as they tripled the number of outlet stores and their profits--while holding on to their best people. Here it is:

Find a Way to Make This Job Fun

The team has created advertising campaigns, store games, and innovative sales--and has redesigned *everything* with flash and color. They believe their battle cry.

Help your team pick the battle cry that will make them winners.

1. Make it a team standard

2. Ask them, "What's the best thing we can do as a team to make a better product (or standard)?"

3. Put it in simple behavioral language that directs an action, such as, "You're in charge of Quality--pull the plug when you have to." Or, "Tell the customer "Yes"-- then find a way to do it." Or, "Be an Info Fanatic! Get the word out to everybody . . . now!"

Want a happy work environment?

Keep a bonfire burning under one great big team goal. The plain fact is, human beings are *happy only when they are striving for something worthwhile.*

"To: All staff. Re: Banzai!"

Simplifying overriding team goals (into a battle cry) in plain language is the most effective thing you can do to insure compliance . . . and is far preferable to issuing dry memos!

Let's play!

Which one of the following battle cries lifted from actual mission statements is a simple call to action, not a useless sermon from the mountaintop?

A. *To provide the highest quality of patient care in the most cost-effective manner.*

B. *To achieve the highest level of excellence in the overall design, manufacture, and distribution of family-oriented greeting cards.*

C. *Stop everything and support the needs of the front line first.*

If you picked either A or B, we respectfully request that you spend a full day in overalls and a name badge working with your people, watching them do what they do.

*We know you'll find that if Hassan, the groundskeeper, Olivia, the press operator, and Manuel, the assistant dining room manager, don't know what specific action is expected of them to accomplish your overriding goal, then **you don't have one.***

Reality check: To be effective, a battle cry must be:

SINCERE
CONSTANT
ATTAINABLE

A familiar "battle cry"

Mary Kay Ash built a $300 million-plus cosmetics business on a single overriding goal:

Do unto others as we would have them do unto us.

The Golden Rule. Sound corny? Ask the scores of women who take it to heart and earn over sixty thousand dollars a year selling her products.

The battle cry doesn't have to be original. It just has to be sincere

> By her own account, Mary Kay first established her battle cry *before* she even had a team or *even knew* what product she wanted to sell. Makes you wonder what's really more important as the motivator--the product or the passion.

Keep it real.

If you like what your team is doing already, make it a battle cry. Shout it so everyone else knows about it

The battle cry that keeps on giving

Avis V.P. Russell James says that Avis workers immediately put on their "We Try Harder" buttons back in '62 and wore them with great pride. He also reported that good work got better and enthusiasm seeped into every corner of the operation. Why? *A team will support a battle cry if they can see an immediate payoff--if it points the way to the winner's circle.*

In 1987 the company became employee-owned after five outside owners in five years. Team members are now wearing a new button: "Now We're Trying Harder Than Ever."

They mean it. Customer complaints are down, complimentary letters are up. So is their stock--up close to 237%.

Why do battle cries work?

Human nature.

> Whatever the human mind
> can hold as a possibility,
> it can achieve in reality.

The more excitement you create around the mind's awareness, the quicker the body moves to make it real.

First, find the behavior you want--then create a raging fire all around it. Visualize it everywhere. Model it. Reward it immediately and feature it in every speech, awards dinner, and annual picnic.

Hire a skywriter and paint the clouds with the battle cry right after you pick it!

Too much excellence can ruin a good thing

Don't be in too much of a hurry to roll out the cannons, strike up the band, and unfurl the banner of "Excellence" as your solution to the battle-cry problem. Noble as it is, excellence is a *result*, not a *process*. Overriding goals should be a journey, not a destination. Your objective is to teach people *how* to climb mountains.

Nobody keeps statistics on the battle cries announced at companies' annual conventions, so we can't speak with absolute statistical authority on our gut feeling that "excellence" has been pretty well burned out as a battle cry. We can say that fifteen of the last seventeen such conventions we've spoken at have announced excellence as their yearly themes on everything from magic crystal paperweights to day-glo shoelaces and premoistened towelettes. This seventeen-company sample encompassed a broad variety of organizations, from national medical associations to women's lingerie manufacturers. (The undergarment folks were very discreet. They passed out expensive black leather attache cases with their gold-embossed logo on the lacy see-through cover flap with the words "Excellence Under It All" printed in shocking pink.)

Push the right button

Very few people are motivated by "excellence." We all want it, but most of us get there by pressing other motivating buttons like *Pride, Praise, Fun, Curiosity, Loyalty, Dedication, Fear,* and *Challenge.*

If Tom Edison's mother had decided simply to press the "Excellence" button, you might be reading these words by candlelight. Tom eventually held the patents on 1,093 inventive pieces of excellence by being . . . curious.

This job should be FUN

Previews of coming attractions

Create excitement before the battle cry is picked. Hold a contest. Make the entries by department, not by individual. Let it be a team function. Pick a big, fun prize--a weekend fun getaway for every member of the winning team, two paid days off, preferential parking, chauffeured limousine to work for a week, etcetera.

How to: Hold a pep rally. Pat folks on the back. Make a point of showing management support for the team's needs. Visualize the prize: use slides, posters, video, and so on. Allow one entry per department. If you don't get what you want, combine two entries into one, add your two cents, and make two awards. It's not important that they come up with the exact battle cry. What's vitally important is that they participate in the birth.

High five on the spot

The recent sports tradition of "high fives" is the most joyful, spontaneous expression of achievement we have. Use it every time a team member models the behavior in the battle cry. This sends an emotional message of accomplishment and recognition to the entire team.

How to: Give everybody permission to do it. Have the managers start the ball rolling every time they see achievement. The most effective demonstration would be to have the CEO do it, even if it's much after the fact. He or she is the model; people will watch for cues.

The behavior you reward is the behavior you'll get. The more emotional the reward, the more often the behavior.

The Light Manager's ACTION check-off ✓

☐ **1. Clarify.**

Define your highest standard to be accomplished in simple behavioral terms. Survey your team; see if they agree. If they don't, incorporate their language.

☐ **2. Make a big production out of it.**

Produce the announcement. Make it a pep rally; fun assembly; lots of balloons and upbeat music. Be sure to say, "This is what *you* want to be our goal, so this is what our goal is."

☐ **3. Measure.**

Decide how to measure how well your team is doing at any given stage; put up a big scoreboard.

☐ **4. Enlist the bigshots.**

Get your CEO on the line to model the behavior--or, if you can't, then scrap the program.

☐ **5. Demonstrate commitment to the new values.**

Reward the behavior loudly and immediately every time you see it. Do it in full view of as much of the world as possible. Fire every manager who doesn't model the behavior. And don't be afraid to let the rest of the team know why.

In the New Reality, Light Managers know . . .

Business desperately needs a reason to give lots of high fives all around.

Picking an overriding goal that, when accomplished, makes your team feel like Winners nurtures self-esteem, the only real productivity strategy there is.

You've got to get their attention. Get passionate. Start a raging fire around your battle cry!

4
COOPERATION
Get action now!

Light Manager's
Profit Strategy #4

I care/ You matter	We're fanatics about cooperating. When you ask for help, we listen and respond.
This job should be fun	Draw your monster and march.

Super Teams cause cooperation by

Stopping all "dumping"

Speaking an "action now" language

Cooperation starts with empowering people to own their own problem

Employees have become experts on "dumping"--delivering problems to their managers, dumping them in their laps, and saying, "Here, you solve them."

Managers in the New Economy don't have time for that. Their job is to empower people to solve their own problems.

> *Every time someone "dumps" a complaint on you, give it back. Say, "What's the best thing you can do to solve it?"*

Stop commiserating--empower!

Ron Smith, A V.P. at Warner Brothers Film Studios, defines losing in the new management environment as spending more than half your time putting out other people's fires, refereeing other people's conflicts, and picking up other people's garbage." Don't collect garbage. Recycle it!

> *In tough times, your job is to make everyone a problem solver. Fortunately, people love this.*

At the General Mills plant in Lodi, California, production shot up forty percent higher than other plants when management asked teams to solve their own problems. At Weaver Popcorn in Indiana, anybody who thinks there's a problem can "pull the plug" on the assembly line. Weaver's quality is among the highest in the international market. New Breed Workers want control. Give it to them!

Super Teams speak a distinctive language of cooperation

They get the other person to say "yes" to something--anything--that starts an action now. They negotiate for cooperation by speaking *action now language*.

When you listen to a Super Team, you will notice that . .

> They *ask for help*
>
> They *state the bottom line simply*
>
> They *offer their best solution*
>
> They *get the other person to agree to do something*

Action now language

Here's how it works. Open up with the four magic words:

"I need your help!"

Start negotiations by putting the other person in a receptive mood. New Breed Workers want to feel they're participating, not just reacting. Saying "I need your help" erases the new resistance to authority. It also sends an immediate message that you're an open, approachable person.

"We have a problem"

The "us vs. them," "labor vs. management" tradition is dead in the New Economy. It divides productivity energy and gets members of the same team thinking of one another as "the enemy." Saying "We have a problem" spotlights the number-one thing we all have to do in difficult times--cooperate or fail. We may never learn to love one another (or even like one another) at work. *But everyone has the obligation to cooperate.* Cooperation--Team Play--is the only way to do more with less and win.

If you have any workers who don't understand that new fact of life, make them aware of that quickly. If they don't buy it, don't waste any time: give them their walking papers.

This Job Should Be Fun

State the problem simply

Don't produce a soap opera. Stop narrating, describing, backgrounding, and embellishing. Cut to the chase! Get to the point quickly. Learn to be a "bottom line communicator." State the issue.

Show the other person you know exactly what the problem is. State it in as few words as possible: "We're one engineering inspector short this month. We can't cover the safety inspections for thirty percent of our equipment."

The longer you take to get to the issue, the less likely you are to win cooperation. Step on the gas!

State why it is crucial

People prioritize everything they hear. They listen and a voice inside says one of two things: "Better do it now," or "It's not crucial, do it later." Your job is to prove why action ought to be taken *now*.

Safety, money, and service gets attention: "Those boilers are very old. If we can't inspect them in time, we could overlook a serious defect, blow an inspection plate, and be faced with a $400,000 repair bill."

"My best solution is . . ."

Here's where you stop the "dumping." Take charge of the problem. State your best answer for the problem. And if people are presenting *you* with problems without taking the initiative to go beyond stating the difficulty and explaining why it's crucial, ask: "What's your best solution?"

Don't allow dumping. Asking for the best solution puts the person on notice to stop, think, and take charge. Dependent employees hold you back in the New Economy. Build independence. Have your people become part of the solution.

"My best solution is to give our remaining two inspectors three hours of overtime for as long as it takes to hire a new person."

"Will you agree to . . ."

Sound the bugle charge. Get the other person to say "yes" to something to start the solution process. Remember, until a person says "yes," no responsibility has been taken. You may get "maybe," "wait and see," "sounds good to me, but . . . " or any number of other phrases that basically translate to "nothing is going to happen." Try again for a direct response: "Will you agree to authorize six hundred dollars in overtime pay to get the job done?"

Management secrets from Bear Bryant, college football's winningest coach:

" I'm just a plowhand from Arkansas, but I have learned how to hold a team together--how to lift some men up, how to calm down others, until finally they've got one heartbeat together, a team. There's just three things I'd ever say: If anything goes bad, I did it; if anything goes semi-good, then we did it; if anything goes real good, then you did it. That's all it takes to get people to win football games for you. **"**

Ask!

Here's the most powerful question you can ask to get a "YES":

> "If I can show you how this can benefit us in terms of [cost savings/quality improvement/greater efficiency], will you agree to consider it?"

"What if the person doesn't agree to my best solution?"

Ask another question that gets the person to say "yes" to something that starts the action process. Unless you're dealing with some extremely incompetent colleague, you can always expect to get a "yes" to something like, "Will you agree to meet tomorrow morning at ten to find ways to work this problem out with me?"

"But what if all I get is 'no' "?

If this happens on a regular basis, you are working in a non-cooperative environment.

Walk.

This job should be FUN

Draw your dragon and march

The reality is you probably face at least one dragon at work, and possibly many more. Dragons are peers and bosses who always give you a hard time when you ask for cooperation.

You can't change them, but you can change how you see them.

Draw that dragon now.

Give it a name: "Harriet the Harpy," "Canyon Mouth Mike," etc.

Store the drawing in a *secure, private place* and guard that place with your life.

Look at the drawing every time you have to confront that person, then tuck it safely away again in your desk.

March in and make your dragon the first person on whom you use your *Action Now* language to get a cooperative "yes."

Once you overcome the biggest intimidating obstacle to your communications, the rest will become routine.

Test yourself. Go for the dragon first!

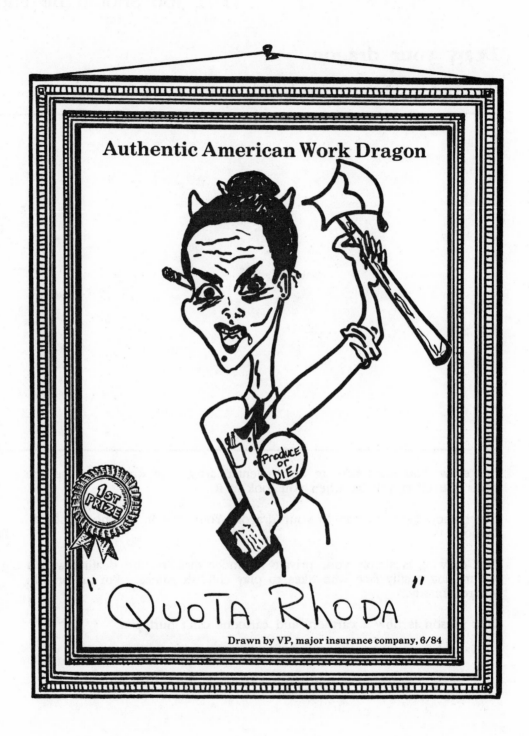

Draw your dragon

Here. Start by defacing this book. What does your dragon look like?

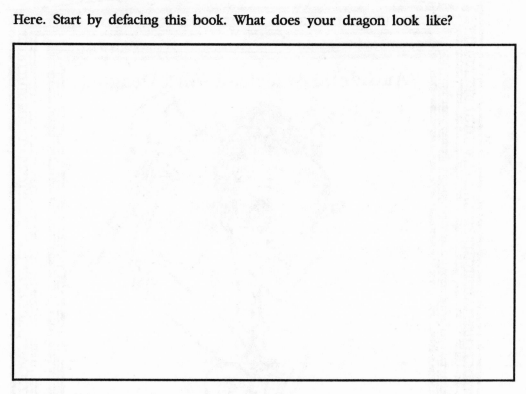

Just draw. You don't have to be a talented artist. The worse you are, the better the effect will be when you look at it.

Never show your cartoon to your dragon. Your dragon has no sense of humor.

This drawing is simply your private reminder that you are dealing with a big kid making a silly face who likes to play childish games: "I'm important; you're nobody."

That person is now a cartoon, and cartoons can't hurt you.

The Light Manager's ACTION check-off

☐ 1. Eliminate "dumping."

Make everybody a problem solver. Accept only solutions.

☐ 2. Talk the right talk.

Use the language of cooperation.

☐ 3. Hold out for results.

Don't leave until you get the other person to agree to a specific action.

In the New Reality, Light Managers know . . .

The New Breed Worker has a desperate need to feel like a winner.

People feel like winners when they sense action toward the goal line. Show it to them.

It is imperative that you stop all "dumping." Ask for their best solutions. Use the language of cooperation.

You yourself must be inclined to say "YES" to something that gets an action underway.

5
GOAL-SETTING:
The "Hot List"

Light Manager's

Profit Strategy #5

I care/ You matter	You know better than the brass what you need to accomplish--so *you* establish what's hot, what's not.
This job should be fun	Post the "Hot List" and bring Dick Tracy, Uncle Sam, and Wonder Woman into the act.

66 Real power is getting people committed. Real power comes from giving it up to others who are in a better position to do things than you are. Control is only an illusion. The only control you can possibly have comes when people are controlling themselves. **99**

Ralph Stayer, CEO
Johnsonville Foods
Sheboygan, Wisconsin

"Take your teambuilding and stuff it!"

During a recent all-day workshop for three hundred registered nurses serving the county of Los Angeles, an angry but eloquent RN interrupted the proceedings. Grabbing the microphone, she expressed the needs of all New Breed Workers:

> "What the hell good is all this teambuilding and empowerment stuff if I'm *not allowed to care for the patients the way I know they should be cared for?* I'm sick of 'upstairs' people telling me how to do what I do best--my job."

Two hundred and ninety-nine nurses stood at this point and applauded. Some were crying. Their spokeswoman continued:

> "Who *are* these people? Have they ever started an IV? Cleaned an infected wound? Hugged a dying patient? Washed blood off their uniforms after every shift? Why are they *telling* me? Why aren't they *asking* me?"

Why not indeed?

The best answer is that they haven't recognized that the sun has set on autocratic management. They don't understand that in tough times only cooperation (I ask you, you ask me, and WE find a solution) pulls teams together.

Case study:
Your team knows best

Re: Good things happen when you let your team pursue what they know is right. (And the proof can be as straightforward as "Spaghetti and pancakes, please.")

Food service personnel at the Squashblossom Restaurant--in Scottsdale, Arizona's four-star Hyatt Regency Hotel--were frustrated. They knew that the only way they could leap from good to extraordinary service was to have complete authority to give the customer anything he or she wanted, whether it was on the menu or not.

They told their supervisor. He *listened*. He said, "Okay, go ahead."

As manager Hal Scott recalls, "Shortly after that meeting, a gentleman came in at 8:30 in the morning and really put our new empowerment to the supreme test. He ordered spaghetti and meatballs for his whole family. He said it was all they could eat for breakfast. Our waiter smiled and said, 'If that's what you want, sir, I'll get it for you.' And he did."

Because Hyatt's supervisors and line communicate so well about what workers believe should be done, the company has adopted what it calls an "Above and Beyond" policy, where every employee has the authority to satisfy the guest's needs on the spot. That's super service from a super team.

The Bottom Line:

> The Squashblossom is continually rated one of the finest restaurants in the west by critics and restaurant goers alike. (Do you think that kind of word-of-mouth helps sales?)

Share power with your producers

There are only three practical ways to empower people.

---

1. Give them something important to do.

2. Give them authority to do it.

3. Back off and let them do it.

MBGOOTW (Management By Getting Out Of The Way)

Corning has organized its workers into 3,000 teams of up to 15 members each. Management has backed off and given its people complete freedom to come up with quality improvement solutions.

Maybe it's a coincidence that Corning's profits have risen 250% since 1982. But we doubt it.

David Lucher, a senior vice president at Corning, says, "By the mid '90s, we'll define good management as the ability to get out of the way."

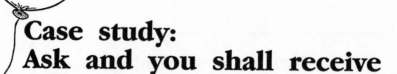

Case study:
Ask and you shall receive

Re: Most managers have no idea what their team really wants.

You'd be surprised what your team really considers urgent. Pat Cruzen, former CEO of the famous Sands Hotel and Casino in Las Vegas, certainly was.

A walk-around kind of manager, Pat had set as his staff's primary goal superior guest service at all levels of the organization. He was particularly concerned about how his hotel operators answered the phone, correctly believing that specific interaction established the "image" of the Sands to a would-be first-time guest.

His private branch exchange (PBX) staff was highly competent--but not overly enthusiastic.

He *asked* the what the number-one goal in their department was.

One wily veteran shattered his lofty aspirations. "What we want," she said, "is sunshine. We need a window. Some of us have been cooped up in this room for over twenty years. There's no daylight in here. It sure would help our enthusiasm a whole lot if we could see the outside world."

On the spot, Pat drew a large cartoon of a window on a sheet of paper, taped it to the wall, and wrote the words "Coming Attraction" for everyone to see. A few weeks later the PBX gang had a real window to the world.

The Bottom Line:

> Your first phone impression of the Sands is brightened considerably by a cheery voice and very courteous assistance.

Let the line decide what's hot--and what's not

We're not talking about long-term goal setting. We're talking about what's *hot*, what's right now, about how to boot the fire eating dragon that's spitting flame at your team this very moment.

> Goals tend to be too lofty. Your work team's problem areas are not in the clouds. They're on the ground, here and now: real, simple, tough, whatever.

When you're doing more with less, you've got to remove the physical and mental obstacles that prevent the team from seeing progress.

The goal in tough times is to get the team to set priorities as far down in the organization as possible to build a strong buy-in. Allow each unit to establish its own "hot list." Don't bring in consultants or look for paperwork to justify it. Just do it!

Call your team together.

Ask them to vote on the top three hot (immediate) problems to solve to move the problem ahead.

Help them by providing a "hot list."

What's a hot list?

It's a list of the twenty-five issues most frequently picked by the working line as the most immediate problems to be solved to increase productivity on the line. (The list that follows was determined by authors' survey of 139 work teams in the manufacturing, information, and service industries over a period of six years.) Let your team add whatever items they want. Everybody has three votes.

Determine the top three. Post them. Ask for three-person teams to come up with the best possible solution to the problem. Whenever possible, give the problem back to the team to be solved and implemented, remembering that . . .

> People work most effectively
> when they believe it's *their* idea,
> not yours.

A list you can present to your team

On the following page are our top twenty-five candidates for your hot list. They were determined by our survey of 139 work teams in the manufacturing, information, and service industries over a period of six years.

What do you, the team, think are the hottest issues--the ones we should tackle first to move ahead?

Check three (3) of the issue you believe should receive immediate attention to improve morale and increase productivity:

___ Better communications between supervisor and front line
___ An explanation of the big picture (Where are we going?)
___ A chance to see how other departments operate
___ Senior management more visible on the front line
___ Appreciation for a job well done
___ To be consulted before major changes take place
___ How are we doing as a business (profit or loss)?
___ To be spoken to with respect
___ More frequent briefing sessions about what's going on around here
___ Physically rearrange the warehouse
___ Settle major personality conflict going on within this division
___ Give everyone in this division an opportunity to say how it should be run
___ More visual proof that we're winning at something
___ Training for all hands on ''Basic People Skills''--how to communicate better for cooperation
___ A big, fun morale booster to bring everybody together
___ Counsel some folks on the need to stop badmouthing, griping, and backstabbing--and start pulling together
___ A chance to be supervisor for a day
___ More attention to producing quality
___ An incentive program
___ Authority to make decisions on my own
___ CEO spending more time on the line chatting with the staff
___ Clear career steps (Where do I go from here?)
___ Encouragement to be the best at one performance function
___ A better way to evaluate performance
___ More informal fun

[add your own below!]

_____

_____

_____

There's nothing wrong with "anonymous"

If you feel the major issues are too sensitive or perhaps may embarrass one of the "problem" people, then call for an anonymous vote.

Why a hot list? Why not a long-term goal-setting session?

Because you're at war. Your people:

- want relief now

- need assurance their ideas count

- want the cynics to stop griping and start cooperating

Establishing just three hot items gives you an opportunity to accomplish the tasks in a shorter period of time and deliver an all-important victory to your team. Remember, in tough times it's important to prove to your people that you are winning at something.

> *"Too many teams approach goal-setting sessions with the same feeling they'd have walking Castle Dracula at midnight. Keep it light, free, and open. People should revel in planning achievement."*
>
> Sandra Schrift, President
> The Podium Speaker's Bureau
> San Diego, California

This job should be FUN

Bring on the superheroes

One large photo processing lab in Buffalo, New York displays its hot "hit list" on a big poster with a large-size folk hero alongside lending support and encouragement that "the deeds will be done." At various times, Dick Tracy, Wonder Woman, and Mighty Mouse have cheered them on to victory.

Fact: Eighty-five percent of today's workers learn what they learn visually. So display your message in a big way, and keep the goals in your workers' line of sight.

Hold a bounce party

Don't tie up your goal-setting sessions with a lot of serious structure. Uptight people don't buy in to other people's goals. Keep it loose, fun, and creative. Green Connection, a plant leasing business in Anchorage, Alaska, has "bounce parties." Someone brings the stir-fried vegetables, and everybody "bounces" ideas off one another. It's particularly effective after you've set the "hot list" to meet and agree on what direction to take.

How to: Limit the meeting to forty-five minutes, tops. Entertain all ideas. The cardinal rule is that no one shoots down anyone else's idea. Add to it or let it fizzle on its own merits. But no negative attacks. You want to encourage openness, not step on it.

Light Manager's ACTION check-off list ✓

☐ 1. Gather the team.

Call your team together. Ask them to vote on the three most important goals to accomplish. Majority rules.

☐ 2. Ask for positive solutions on each goal.

Ask for positive solutions on each. Agree on one. If you can't, appoint a three-person action team to come up with one.

☐ 3. Post the problems.

You now have a team agenda.

☐ 4. Make everyone a consultant.

Ask every day how to achieve results.

☐ 5. Celebrate victory.

Go bananas when the priorities are accomplished. Jump! Holler! Praise! Reward! Get the big guns from upstairs to come down and congratulate the troops.

☐ 6. Start again.

Vote for the next "Big Three."

In the New Reality, Light Managers know . . .

New Breed Workers have a desperate need for control. All around them, bosses are frustrating that need by imposing, controlling, and dictating goals.

When you give people permission to work on *their* hot issues, you're placing them in the highest zone of possible achievement: self-determination.

6
ROTATION
Exchange Combatants

Light Manager's
Profit Strategy #6

I care/ **You matter**	We know you need better cooperation to make your work easier. Go work in another function for awhile and tell us what to do.
This job **should** **be fun**	Start a Moccasin Program.

Boredom--a fate worse than death

"Every evil can be traced back to boredom," said historian Alexis de Tocqueville. He may have been the first business consultant and not known it.

Your workers are bored.

Work is unreal to them. Only the weekends, where all the "action" lies, matter.

> "Oh, get real! I'm a manager, not a social director. If a worker is bored, that's his or her problem. The business of business is business."

Wrong on all counts.

If a worker is bored, he or she has the ultimate power to sabotage your quest for excellence--*the power to be mediocre.* The business of business *used* to be business. Now the business of business is:

Basic education
Drug and alcohol counseling
Values training
Conflict resolution
Self-esteem building
Day care
Social directing

Why? Because your productivity depends on a satisfied worker.

116

Rotate, rotate, rotate

Give your team the opportunity to see how every part of the whole functions. Exchange workers from different departments and let them perform the other person's tasks for a while.

The best way to cement cooperation is to experience just how hard the rest of the team is pulling on the same rope.

Here's what a rotation program will do for you:

> *Create* excitement
> *Reduce* inter-departmental conflict
> *Help* team members detect flaws in each other's work
> *Make you think* and apply problem-solving techniques to new situations

How to set it all up

Start small. Run a pilot program. Here's the game plan.

---

1. Exchange combatants. Get agreement from the manager of a department you are having some trouble with to exchange workers for one day.

2. Ask for a volunteer. If you don't get one, pick one of your marginal producers. It's a gamble, but if he or she comes back with enthusiasm, you've gone a good way toward selling the program to your resident gang of doubting Thomases.

3. No paperwork, please. Just call the team together and let the rotated worker tell what he saw and felt.

Case study: Trading places

Re: The day the city of Long Beach, California sent its top managers packing . . .

Can a deputy police officer become the director of community planning overnight and be effective? Can the human resource manager take over the city jail at a moment's notice without also taking a heavy dose of tranquilizers? Can fifty percent of the top managers in one of the best-run cities in America change jobs without any preparation and keep the fifth-largest municipality of America's largest state from turning into Pee-Wee's Playhouse?

Yep! They could--and they did--in the fall of 1984. Listen to Bill Storey, former deputy police chief, and now back at his regular job (Director of Personnel).

"We were having some conflict between departments," explains Storey, "and the City Manager felt we all ought to change places and find out firsthand how the other half really lived and worked."

Every manager to be rotated was nervous--and with good cause. There was no formal training, no discussion, no preparation. Just "Do it--you'll find a way." They did. And then a wonderful thing happened: cooperation.

"We didn't know a thing about our jobs," Storey continues, "so we had to ask our new staffs for help. They loved it. It gave them a chance to take charge, make suggestions they knew would be listened to and be immediately appreciated."

Charlie Clark, the police chief (now retired) who became a community developer, smiled and echoed the sentiments of ninety-four percent of the managers who participated in the rotation: "It was the best work experience I ever had."

"There were lots of problems," Storey explained, "between myself and the department before the rotation. Now I have the greatest respect for them--and they know I put my pants on the same way they do in the morning. It was great fun."

The Bottom Line:

> Inter-department cooperation improved noticeably; conflict with a union leader ended amicably.

Rotating workers does a lot more than break the cycle of boredom

It makes work more satisfying and unlocks hidden talent and vitality within your team.

At General Motors' Detroit Gear and Axle plant, a team of thirty workers cross-trained from other departments, built parts for rear-wheel drive suspension systems, and cut warranty costs by *four hundred percent* in just two years.

The wave is coming--ride it!

In a reductionist economy, where every resource is being compacted, thinned out, and asked to serve many masters, it is inevitable that "multi-skilling," cross-training, and cross-functional teams will rise to the top.

It's the logical use of limited human resources.

Don't wait for the boss to paddle out to you

Ride the wave to him or her! Start the program at your level Let the success swell from the bottom to the top.

Light Manager's notebook

Re: Maybe there's only one way to get your team to appreciate the customer's point of view: switch places!

Employees of the 180 branches of the Meridian banking group in Pennsylvania were recently trained to get "a better feel" for handicapped customers. They had to fill out deposit slips with Vaseline smeared on their glasses and count money with three fingers on each hand taped together.

The idea was to give them a better understanding of what older customers with glaucoma or arthritis may be going through. It worked!

The Bottom Line:

A heightened sensitivity to the needs of older customers-- resulting in a substantial increase in new accounts.

This job should be FUN

Start a Moccasin Program

Keep the program light and free of bureaucratic entanglements.

> *"Don't judge any man until you have walked two moons in his moccasins."*
> Native American proverb

Buy a pair of Indian moccasins and hang them up where your team can see them and be reminded of the importance of cooperation.

Refer to them when your team member reports back from his or her rotation.

Give out fun moccasin awards at the end of the year--one to the team member from another department who displayed exceptional cooperation and one to your own team member who made a contribution to the visited team.

A gift certificate for a pair of shoes would be a nice gift for each of these contributors.

Shadow the boss

Hyatt Hotels has a fun program called National Hyatt In Touch Day, where selected top brass have an employee from the line "shadow" them all day long just to get the feel of the team problems from the top. Even the president gets a shadow.

The Light Manager's ACTION check-off

☐ **1. Start small.**   Rotate one worker.

☐ **2. Target.**   Target the department or division from whom you need the most cooperation as your "rotation partner."

☐ **3. Ask.**   When your rotated employee comes back, ask him or her only one question: "How can we work together better?"

☐ **4. Broadcast.**   Let everybody know the results.

☐ **5. Act!**   Implement an immediate suggestion to "make things better."

In the New Reality, Light Managers know . . .

You can't just talk cooperation--you've got to demonstrate it. And people learn most effectively when you allow them to experience the learning themselves.

7
LITIGATION:
Resolve all conflict
in the boo-boo stage

Light Manager's
Profit Strategy #7

I care/ You matter	I recognize you feel wronged and I want to solve your problem immediately.
This job should be fun	Track all ouches!

66 Fun on the job, caring relationships, and humane treatment is the antidote to employee lawsuits. **99**

Burt Pines, Senior Partner
Alschuler, Grossman and Pines

Resolve all conflict in the boo-boo stage

Employee lawsuits are out of control. They cost employers more than twenty billion dollars a year to litigation attorneys--and that doesn't include the costs of settlements and judgments!

The whole ugly process shatters employee trust, tarnishes reputations, and eats up an enormous amount of time and talent.

Most such lawsuits are completely avoidable.

A recent survey of corporate attorneys indicates that . . .

> THE BIGGEST CULPRIT in most workplace legal actions is the frontline supervisor. Rather than working out problems amicably, he or she gets bent out of shape and reacts with hostility.

Managers cause litigation. Managers can prevent it.

Put up a caring "prevent defense"

In football jargon, a "prevent defense" is when you pull back and give your opponent plenty of room in front of you in order to prevent that team's going "beyond your defenses" to score.

129

A caring prevent defense means . . .

. . . being familiar with employee rights.

. . . dealing with problems immediately.

. . . becoming a super listener.

. . . plugging the complainer into a fair problem-solving program.

. . . avoiding retaliation or retribution.

Be familiar with employee rights

The result of employees' taking the boss to court is a new body of law being written about what you can and cannot do in certain circumstances. The more cases you face, the more "dos" and "don'ts" you, the manager, have to contend with.

Mr. P., the CEO of a large manufacturing company in Tulsa, Oklahoma, obviously wasn't aware of what constitutes sexual harassment in today's workplace. He kept leaving single roses on his married secretary's desk, wrapped in notes that said, "From your secret admirer." She sued. And won $250,000. The board of directors fired him.

Know their rights. See the section at the end of this book entitled "Light Manager's Guide to Hot Legal Issues."

Deal with problems immediately

Swift attention to complaints shows care. John A. Smith, CEO of Sports A'Foot, had a "red phone" put in his office so any employee could call him directly to discuss grievances his people at lower levels seemed unable to resolve satisfactorily. Allowing free, open access to the boss has worked. Not one of his 350 employees has felt the need to go to court.

Think of your children. When they fall or scrape their knees, they cry out, run to Mommy, and demand miraculous healing immediately.

You can't heal, but you can soothe. Usually that's enough to prevent boo-boos from becoming major surgery.

66 We don't tolerate angry or irate, tyrannical bosses. We isolate them, sit them down, discuss the problem, make that person change . . . If they don't change, we get rid of them. 99

Terry Bean, VP Human Resources
Federal Express

The sun has set on autocratic managers!

Become a superior listener

People perceive your level of care by how well you listen to them. How much your employee perceives you care determines how far he or she will go with their complaint.

Studies on the recent rash of medical malpractice suits indicate that physicians who know their patients well and are perceived as good listeners are less likely to be sued. "Many malpractice suits come about because people are angry at their doctors for not communicating," says Cornell's Dr. David Rogers, former dean of Johns Hopkins Medical College.

> A good Light Manager assumes the doctor-patient relationship with the complaining team members and listens attentively, even to the chronic complainers.

Listen, listen, listen

How? Keep an *open mind*. Make *soft eye contact*; don't stare. Forget self; concentrate on *what* they say, not how they say it. Ask *"why questions"* to get more information. Keep saying *"I understand"* and nod your head as you do. Say, *"What would you like me to do to help?"* *Contact them yourself* and tell them your decision.

News flash!

*"Ashland Oil Company was ordered today to pay over **sixty million dollars** to former vice-presidents who were judged to be the victims of wrongful discharge."*

*"The Oregon State Supreme Court yesterday upheld an award of **$20,000** in benefits to Sheriff Harry A. McGarrah, who attributed his acute depression to harassment by his supervisor."*

*"Three whistle-blowing employees who were fired by Lockheed Corporation yesterday filed suit against the company for **fifteen million dollars**. The case is expected to be among the most expensive employee lawsuits to defend in American legal history."*

Your employees read headlines, too. They know . . .

The courts are siding with workers.

If they don't get immediate satisfaction, the "easy answer" is: Sue the boss!

Their chances of winning are great.

Plug the complainer into a fair problem-solving process

And give it a "soft" name. "Grievance procedure" implies continued hostility. Lighten up!

Bank of America calls its program "Let's Talk."

An employee can raise any concerns he or she hasn't been able to deal with effectively with his or her manager to thirty personnel specialists hired specifically to protect employee rights. They have a backup process called "Open Line."

Any concern the employee has can be written up in a memo and given to an Open Line coordinator. The coordinator will anonymously present the employee's letter to the appropriate level of management, who must respond within ten days.

Make the process easy, open, available, and free of intimidation. Cut the red tape.

Talk about cost effective programs! Federal Express has a Guaranteed Fair Treatment Program that is worth millions to that company's bottom line. Their overall civil lawsuits and wrongful terminations are the lowest in corporate America. Why?

They mean what they say. Employees have the right to appeal their complaint right up to the Chairman of the Board (and he listens).

If the present "litigation madness" phase continues along the same course, by the year 2000 half the citizens of the country will be suing one another. The other half will probably be trying to get into law school.

The Light Manager's secret weapon

Learning to criticize positively.

Your object is to tell someone something is wrong without destroying his self-esteem.

The trick is to place the criticism within a context of positive reinforcement.

BEGIN WITH TWO POSITIVE REINFORCEMENTS

"You really are a very savvy veteran."

"You have the skills to do this job well."

INSERT YOUR CRITICISM

"I wish WE could find a way to solve the problem of _____ ."

ADD ONE MORE POSITIVE REINFORCEMENT

"I know you can handle this change easily."

FINISH WITH A RAY OF HOPE

"If WE work on this thing together, I know WE can build a stronger cooperation."

NEGATIVE CRITICISM DESTROYS SELF-ESTEEM AND WINS YOU LIFELONG ENEMIES. ABANDON IT. IT DOESN'T MAKE PEOPLE BETTER.

Resource: "The Universal Traveler," by Don Koberg and Jim Bagnall; William Kaufmann, Inc., San Francisco.

This job should be FUN

Track your ouches

Tiny ouches have a habit of getting bigger and more irritating if you don't put a band-aid on them quickly. And they seem to get bigger and more hurtful in direct proportion to a lack of attention.

People in pain are like kids with a boo-boo; they need you to notice and say, "I'm sorry you're hurt. There, there. Everything's going to get better. Now, don't worry."

You show extraordinary care by being constantly aware of need. Remind yourself of that. Put a band-aid on your desk. Write on it the name of the person who has the "ouch." Track that ouch every day until the boo-boo is gone.

Darryl DuBois, a general manager of a large insurance agency in Atlanta, sticks the band-aids to his phone--and doesn't remove them until all his "First Aid" efforts have relieved the problem.

His people look at those band-aids and know the boss cares. The band-aid method also keeps a potentially explosive situation on the lighter, more manageable side of life.

The Light Manager's ACTION check-off

☐ 1. Stay abreast.

Read The Light Manager's Guide to Hot Legal Issues (see the end of this book). Keep it handy for ready reference.

☐ 2. Intercept.

Spot all conflict in the boo-boo stage.

☐ 3. Go looking for trouble.

If the complainer doesn't come to you, go to the complainer. Use the magic words: "How can I help?"

☐ 4. Don't defend the company.

Defend fair play.

In the New Reality, Light Managers know . . .

Showing extraordinary care to your people's hurts--real or imagined--is the best way to prevent litigation.

To deal successfully with the more legally aware New Breed Workers, you cannot afford to hire or keep managers who abide by the master/servant relationship.

Authoritarianism is dead! The laws protect employees against it.

You must immediately resolve problems by treating the employee with dignity, honesty, and respect.

First aid is very often the best aid.

8
EVALUATIONS
Turn the Tables

Light Manager's
Profit Strategy #8

I care/ You matter	We really do value your opinions. Let's turn the tables on evaluations. Tell the bosses how *they're* doing.
This job should be fun	Make it a "Mutual Do-It-Yourself" project.

You can't go around calling your folks a "family" or a "team" and then treat them like pupils. If you give them a report card, *let them give you one.*

Tradition should work for the team, not against it

The employee evaluation has been a time-honored tradition. But does it work any more in the new "participative" environment?

Is it consistent to shout, "We need everybody's input on how to make everything better around here," and then not allow the team to tell the coaches how they're doing?

> *" There is no one in the company more knowledgeable about my performance as a manager than the people I manage."*

Mary Isom
Shift supervisor
BASF Corporation

Remember the bottom line

Light Managers get more from their teams because they prove they believe in two-way communication. Letting your team evaluate you is the strongest message you can send; it shows that you value their opinion.

Turn the table. Mean what you say about more team involvement.

" Sure, we have the fun of volleyball games, lots of parties, trips to Disneyland, and weenie roasts. But the real fun is getting up in the morning and coming to an environment that constantly acknowledges and rewards your contribution. Our fun is totally involving our team in the challenge of making a better product . . . and a lot of times, letting them create a new one. Our managers put pride and people before profit, and our folks know that. That'll keep a smile on your face long after the volleyball game is over. **"**

Rick Ralston, CEO
Crazy Shirts, Honolulu, Hawaii

"They review me? Isn't this opening Pandora's Box?"

Just a little. Sure, some people will use their "new power" to "get even" with a supervisor with whom they're having difficulty. Sure, it will tend to be more subjective than objective in the beginning. But so what?

You accept the pain in the birthing process because the end result is so joyful.

Success keys to allowing your team to evaluate you

Prepare your managers for an initial shock (most managers have no idea how they affect their team).

Don't get personal. Ask people to evaluate how the boss cooperates.

Make it simple.

Make it anonymous.

It's not what your people say--it's how you react to it

Light Manager Rick Ralston is the CEO of Crazy Shirts in Hawaii. He's the creative entrepreneur who started the whole designed T-shirt craze in the United States. He's build a fifty-million-dollar business listening and acting on employee evaluations and suggestions. Put simply, he treats every one of his 600 employees as if they were valued customers. Rick shows immediate response to employee criticisms. He doesn't care if someone is criticizing the company or a specific supervisor within it. He just listens, evaluates, and acts appropriately.

What should the evaluation form look like?

It should be simple, practical, short, and to the point. It should not exceed one sheet of paper.

We highly recommend the communications categories developed by Huseman, Hatfield, and Gatewood in 1978. In light of the new emphasis on participation, it is even more relevant today. We added a rating system to create the following worksheet.

My Supervisor:	Always	Often	Some-times	Never
POSITIVE EXPRESSION				
Strikes up casual conversations with me				
Jokes good naturedly with me				
DIRECTION				
Tells me what materials and equipment to use when doing my work				
Tells me what steps to follow when doing my work				
RATIONALE				
Tells me what tasks are to be done				
Tells me the reasons for company policies				
NEGATIVE EXPRESSION				
Criticizes my work in front of others				
Ridicules or makes fun of me				
INFORMATION				
Informs me about company rules and policies				
Informs me about future plans for my work group				
PARTICIPATION				
Asks me for suggestions about how work should be done				
Asks me for my opinions				
FEEDBACK				
Lets me know when I have done a good job				
Lets me know how I compare with my fellow workers				

(To maximize the effect of the evaluation process, let the supervisor evaluate himself before you show him the evaluations of employees. Then have him compare evaluations; ask what needs improving with regard to team perception of the supervisor.)

Psst!

You can go out and pay a few thousand dollars do have an employee evaluation form made up by a consultant. Or you can use the Crazy Shirts, Inc. form provided at the end of this book. Free is more fun.

Keep the evaluation ball rolling; go all the way

Let the team evaluate the company. Do it once a year. Don't be bashful: post the results!

Promise to work on the improvement areas. Ask for everybody's help. When you achieve better results on the next survey, congratulate the team! Tell them we're getting better.

If you've got fifty employees or less, capitalize on your informality. Hornall Anderson Design Works in Seattle holds "Performance Discussions" to solidify the team concept. They evaluate group--not individual--effort.

Management and the line sit informally and . . .

>   *discuss team strengths and shortcomings*
>   *evaluate management support*
>   *target immediate improvements*

This is a very exciting approach to teambuilding. It stimulates open communications, focuses on team accomplishments, and removes the intimidation most people feel when they're asked to evaluate another person.

Case study: Do you stink?

Re: Having the guts to listen and act.

> *"You think, 'I've done all this for (the employees) and they think I'm a jerk who doesn't care. You have to realize: maybe they're right."*

> Keith Dunn, Partner
> McGuffey's Restaurant Chain

It's particularly hard when you've been passionately preaching you are an employee-oriented business to learn that many of your 220 employees think you stink. That's what Keith found out when he read his team's first evaluation of management.

After the smoke cleared from his nostrils, he realized how he had to respond: Don't debate your team's negative perceptions--deal with them. It's their reality!

Keith listened to his team, which was telling him, essentially, "You're shoving too many programs down our throats." They had better ideas. The dining room staff wanted a say in the making of the menus. They also wanted to change their uniforms and have fun on dress-up days (everyone wears a costume). They wanted M-I-B Teams, too.

They got it all.

The Bottom Line:

> Profits have increased forty
> percent a year while turnover
> has dropped below 48%--one-fifth
> the industry average.

This job should be FUN

Make it a "do-it-yourself" project

If you're after self-determination to get your team really motivated, then give them the tools.

Let them evaluate themselves. It's a great way to cement trust. Here's how it works. They fill out the form. The manager sits face to face with each team member, and together they agree to target areas for improvement.

Do this at least every ninety days. The quicker the cycle time, the quicker the Team member has to see improvement. Caution: The manager should not upgrade or downgrade an item unless the team member agrees. Otherwise you have no "buy in" to improvement.

Manager, mirror thyself!

If you want to "soften the blow" of the team's evaluating you, start off with a more informal, fun self-evaluation. Fill out the form on the next page. Copy it and hand it to your team. If they agree, they keep it. If they don't, they fill in the additional boxes and leave it on your desk.

DEAR TEAM . . .

I'm looking at myself through your eyes. If you disagree, check off the boo-boo areas and leave it on my desk. I'd appreciate it. You need not sign this form unless you want to.

_____
(Manager's Name)

What three things about me would you want to change? (Please circle.)

Pat me on the back more often

Listen to me more often

Stop hounding me

Let me make suggestions

Leave me on my own

Smile once in a while

Ask me how I feel

Stop trying to prove to me how smart you are

Stop yelling

Stop talking down to me

Stop flirting

Stop being so aloof

Dress neater

Let me know what's going on with management

Train me

Give me a challenge

Take an interest in my work

Other suggestions:

_____

_____

The Light Manager's ACTION check-off

☐ 1. Put together a team evaluations form.

The form should address your performance, and should be based on leadership and cooperation skills, not personality traits. (See examples.)

☐ 2. Make it simple.

Most evaluations look like they're an addendum to your income tax returns.)

☐ 3. Make it anonymous.

Keep the pressure off.

☐ 4. Don't schedule it close to your evaluation of them.

You want the most accurate information you can get your hands on.

☐ 5. Make it public.

Announce to the team what areas they said you had to work on. (It takes guts, but it's a small price to pay for the trust you'll get in return.)

In the New Reality, Light Managers know . . .

How your team perceives you is the key to how well they "buy in" to your goals.

It is pointless to disagree with negative perceptions. Accepting them is the best course of action. Your team's perceptions are their reality, and they have to deal with their reality, not yours, if you're going to increase their productivity.

154

9
TRAINING:
Stick to the Golden Rule

**I care/
You matter**

You tell us what
people skills you need
to improve your
relationships with your
team, and we'll give
them to you.

**This job
should
be fun**

Use "Inside
Consultants."

66 Listen. If your supervisor is a sonofabitch, all the other T.L.C. stuff coming down from the front office doesn't mean a damn thing. And do me a favor. Don't print my name. I might get fired. **99**

Metal worker
Chicago, Illinois

Train frontline supervisors to think straight, talk nice, and listen good

Sounds kind of demeaning, doesn't it? We don't intend it to be. It's just that we've consulted with hundreds of corporations on personnel problems. Invariably, we've found that . . .

EVERY MORALE PROBLEM, communication bottleneck, drop in quality, and high rate of absenteeism can be traced to the closed door of a supervisor who's never been trained how to get people to do things together--to talk nicely, think, listen, and have the patience of a saint.

How important is the supervisor to your productivity picture?

He or she *is* the whole picture.

Newby and Robinson, in their classic 1983 study, found:

> **The use of individual feedback and reinforcement from supervisors increased workers' efficiency in all job areas.**

Behr and Love (1983) went a step further in their conclusions:

> **System rewards and positive feedback have the greatest impact on worker productivity.**

If you want to do something about worker productivity, you want--by definition--to do something about supervisor feedback.

Let's get real

Your New Breed workers don't believe a damn thing you say about teamwork until they see the proof close up. Your team doesn't work for the company. It works for one underpaid, undertrained, overstressed supervisor who is the real key to any million-dollar strategy you may gaze at on your computer screen.

If that supervisor hasn't got the communications skills to build extraordinary cooperation--or if he or she is a sonofabitch--you're dead in the water.

TRAINING: Stick to the Golden Rule

And what kind of workforce is your supervisor communicating to?

The Armageddon Index

Drugs. One in every 20 workers uses drugs regularly. One out of every four of those steals as a result of drug abuse. Six out of ten of those employees who use drugs sell drugs to coworkers. *Cost:* An estimated $33 billion annually in lost productivity, morale problems, and absenteeism. (Survey by Runzheimer International.)

Alcohol. One out of four workers is an alcoholic or has an alcohol-related problem. Forty percent of all workplace fatalities are due to alcohol. Forty-seven percent of all serious injuries on the job are due to alcohol. *Cost:* $65 billion annually in lost productivity, morale problems, and absenteeism. (Survey by Runzheimer International.)

Wasted time. Two months of the average worker's year is wasted. That's one-sixth of the year--completely unproductive. *Cost:* $150 billion in lost time. (Survey by Robert Half, International.)

Sickness. One million workers call in sick every day. *Cost:* $1.4 billion a day, based on a yearly total of 330 million workdays actually lost. (Survey by Health Insurance Association of America.)

Illiteracy. Approximately 30% of all secretaries have difficulty with job-level reading requirements; 50% of managers and supervisors cannot write a paragraph that is free of grammatical errors; 50% of all workers (skilled and unskilled) cannot solve simple math problems. *Cost:* $5 to $10 billion yearly spent on basic literacy training. (Surveys by Public Resource and Basic Skills in the Workplace.)

Litigation. Two-thirds of all civil litigation filed in Los Angeles during a recent two-month period were wrongful termination suits. *Cost:* Over $100,000 per disgruntled worker, since employees win two-thirds of the time at an average plaintiff award level of $177,000. (Study by Rand Corporation.)

There's more. New hires today lack fundamental social skills (like how to speak courteously to a customer or coworker). That unsettling trend was noted by Edward Herman, president of the American Express North American Travel Related Services division, in a June 1990 article in *Fortune*. The same story reported that at Super Valu's Cub Food Markets in Denver, supervisors must teach workers how to stand and walk erectly and must even remind some of them to dress for work with shoes tied and shirts ironed.

Get real! This isn't basic stuff. It's potty training! And the job of changing those diapers falls to your supervisor.

Light Manager's Notebook

Re: Open a "Leadership College"!

The super success of the Super Team at Scandinavian Air System, (SAS) led by CEO Jan Carlson, has been heralded many times over. Carlson took over an airline that had lost millions; twenty-four months later he recorded a very high profit picture indeed. He did it by emphasizing teamwork as the highest management goal--and by giving his pilots, stewardesses, counter reps, secretaries, and maintenance personnel the authority to improve quality on the spot.

SAS now believes that to maintain a high cooperation level they must train all supervisors in the basic communications skills that keep winning teams ahead of the pack. They've opened SAS Leadership College for everybody. Courses include internal motivation, external motivation, human resources, and their new "winner"--Internal Marketing: learning how to get your team to work with you.

Has all this had any effect on the supervisors? Eileen Drutman, marketing development manager for SAS, says, "It has affected the very nature of how we conduct meetings--and it greatly facilitates the communications flow, both internally and externally. Leadership talent has evolved."

SUGGESTION: If you should decide to open a Leadership College at your organization, you might give some serious thought to renaming it Superior Cooperation Training, or "Golden Rule" Training. That's the central survival strategy you want to keep constantly in front of your team: WE ONLY WIN BY INCREASING COOPERATION.

What kind of training?

There are hundreds of prepackaged leadership training programs glutting the corporate education market. Most human resource directors spend a good deal of their time sorting them out, listening to snazzy sales presentations, and reading reams of high-tech-designed marketing material that promises everything this side of immortality.

A few of these programs are quite good. Most, however, are too remote from your team's specific trench warfare to make a lasting impression. Don't use any of them unless they give your supervisors exactly what they say they need.

Most general leadership training is too general. *You* design the training. Call it a "What Kind of Skills Would You Like To Improve" survey.

> *Survey all your supervisors. Ask them what specific leadership skills they would like to develop to make their work more effective.*
>
> *Make certain you don't make it look like an evaluation.*
>
> *Survey the people who work for them and ask them the same questions.*
>
> *Don't get bureaucratic. Stay away from phrases like "Training Needs Assessment."*

Case study: Self-determination reaps big rewards

Re: Participating in your own improvement is fun . . . and very productive.

Mercy Hospital and Medical Center in San Diego has a Super Team of 2,000 employees. It wasn't always thus. Front line supervisors used to have the lowest performance ratings in the organization. No more. Light Manager Mary Yarbrough, chief operating officer, and Lisa Carroll, training director, asked the team what they needed. Then they designed a program to fit, and allowed people to, as Lisa puts it, "plug themselves into the workshops they needed."

"The fact that people could choose their own improvement path," Lisa continues, "made all the difference in the world. Relationships improved, enthusiasm returned, people are having fun." One supervisor commented: "The training changed my life."

And that's precisely what effective training *should* do.

We want YOU to design the next training.
What kind of skills would you like to improve?

We all know that the only way to win in difficult times is to beef up those skills that bring us together and build stronger cooperation.

Please tell us what skills you would like to improve, and we'll make sure you get them in our upcoming training programs.

DIRECTIONS: Please use the key below to determine the number that best describes how strongly you feel you need training in the given area. Write the number next to the training category. <u>Please</u> <u>be</u> <u>honest.</u>

> 5 (Definitely want training)
> 3 (Would be helpful)
> 1 (Not really necessary)
> 0 (No need)

PROBLEM SOLVING
How to:
a. Define a problem __
b. Gather facts __
c. Look for solutions __
d. Choose an effective solution __
e. Involve the team in solutions __
f. Make a final decision __

COMMUNICATING FOR COOPERATION
How to:
g. Praise good work __
h. Criticize poor work __
i. Properly give an order __
j. Delegate authority __
k. Solve personality conflicts __
l. Listen to gripes __
m. Ask for help __

n. Respect others' feelings __
o. Motivate different personalities __
p. Speak clearly __
q. Set goals __
r. Involve the team in major decisions __
s. Discipline __
t. Find out what the team expects of me __
u. Be open, approachable __
v. Set operating standards __
w. Recognize personal problems __
x. Celebrate victories __
y. Have fun __

Please list here the letters of the three most important skills for you to learn:_____

"That's too simple; too naive!"

Consider this. Almost all the major fast food chains have put pictures of their hamburgers, french fries, and shakes *on the cash register keys* because, as one Cherry Hill, New Jersey, store manager explained, "If we didn't, we wouldn't be able to get enough help to stay open." The point is, you may be surprised by the challenges your managers are actually facing, and the attendant demands that will be made upon them.

"Sure, we hire the handicapped and senior citizens," the fast-food store manager continued, "but not for humanitarian reasons. More often than not, they're the only applicants who can read and count to ten." If he was overstating his problem, it wasn't by much.

According to the U.S. Bureau of Labor Statistics, sixty-seven percent of new hires in the next two years will not be able to write a complex sentence, or read well enough to understand the instruction manuals of the machines they operate. It just may be that, before you start teaching people how to think ahead and how to treat customers, you should take a critical look at your team and get even simpler. You may have to teach people *how to read and write.*

"We already know their needs. What's the point?"

Participation is the point. "Buy-in" is the point. People work most effectively when they believe it's their idea, not yours. Remember, this is the New Breed Worker. The survey is a powerful tool for you to send the message that motivates: I CARE--YOU MATTER. You tell me what you want, and I get it for you. It's called empowerment.

Super Teams like Nabisco Co., in Hanover, New Jersey, call it listening to the front line and acting immediately to get them what they want. They frequently form employee task groups to determine what training the people on the line feel they need.

> Unfortunately, you can't expect your supervisors to understand or even be receptive to participative team building. They've been brought up in the "give-orders-cover-your-tail-stay-on-people's-backs-till-the-job's-done" school of supervision. They've got to be taught a new way.

167

Look who's really educating America

In Armonk, New York, IBM is spending $900 million a year to educate and train employees. That's slightly more than the annual budget of Harvard University.

IBM teaches everything from robotics to proper communication with customers and coworkers. And IBM is not alone.

Every year, corporate America spends $200 billion dollars training its employees. That's roughly comparable to all the money spent in this country on secondary and college learning. Much of the money is spent to train workers things many of them should have learned as children. But it has to be done.

> *When a team falters, a good coach goes back to basics. That's always the beginning of the apparently "miraculous" comeback.*

This job should be FUN

Use "Inside Consultants"

Stop spending big bucks and embarrassing your staff trainer by bringing in slick outside consultants who tell you how to do what they couldn't do when they held down 9-to-5 jobs (and charge you three times as much as they used to earn). Use people your employees already know and respect. Use local heroes. Use "inside consultants." The 16,000 employees of Godfather Pizza love the president's gung-ho humor so much that they've asked *him* to make the training tapes. The tapes are the biggest hit they've ever had.

Make home videos

Off-the-shelf training can cost you from $7,000 to over $300,000. And what do you get? A fat workbook that reads like the Dead Sea Scrolls and videos that belong on Pee Wee's Playhouse. In short, you get a lot of razzmatazz and fancy footwork that has no relationship to the stuff your front line actually has to face.

Most training insults the intelligence of your workers. They know it's not real. They know it doesn't fit.

Take that video camera in the PR Department or the one sitting in the back of the training office, select your team superstars, and shoot *your* reality.

Nabisco frequently uses its own employees as "TV stars" in this way; it wins interest and acceptance for the material being presented as a result.

Light Manager's ACTION check-off

☐ 1. Change the approach.

Target every front-line supervisor for "thinking" and "talking" boot camp.

☐ 2. Survey.

Ask them what they want to improve. And survey the people who work for them and ask them the same thing.

☐ 3. Use "Inside Consultants."

Look around for "in-house" superstars who can do the training. You've got plenty. Find them.

☐ 4. Beware of the experts.

Don't buy "off-the-shelf" training until a live person comes to see you and agrees to modify the training to give you exactly what you and your team ask for.

☐ 5. Gather the VIPs.

Have every supervisor's manager attend the entire training. He or she has no more important job than to show support for his or her most critical player. Get the CEO to attend the opening sessions of all the training. If he or she is too busy to attend, look for a new job, because you're working for a phony. Managing in the New Reality is all about showing extraordinary care for the things that matter most to the front line.

In the New Reality, Light Managers know . . .

The communication between supervisor and line is your most crucial relationship, because it's where the "action" of the business takes place. It's where product/service and customer meet for profit or loss.

That relationship is defined by how your supervisor talks and listens to the line.

Put the coping-with-cholesterol seminars on hold and give your hard-pressed trench commanders the simple tools they need to lead people--thinking, talking, and listening.

10
WORKSPACE:
Provide a "Green Light"
Environment

Light Manager's
Profit Strategy #10

I care/ You matter	We want you to feel your environment has an open, free, comfortable atmosphere.
This job should be fun	Color the park.

Red light, green light

It's the workers' experience with their immediate physical environment that allows their creativity to flow. They look at the space and read signs. Those signs can say one of two things.

GREEN LIGHT: "Yes, we want you to feel free to open up, ask questions, take charge, find new ways."

RED LIGHT: "No, we don't want that."

Why should a Light Manager be so concerned with the physical environment?

Isn't it enough to keep it clean, safe, and well-lighted, with the thermostat set at sixty-eight degrees? After all, for fifty years, people worked pretty successfully in windowless grey caves sitting in a green metal chair at a brown desk. Why change?

Because *your people have changed.*

Because *the things that make the New Breed Worker happy are vastly different from what made Grandma and Grandpa content.*

Because *environment is a key determinant of behavior, and you've got to maximize every people-productivity factor you have.*

Remember your challenge. You are managing a paradox: create a highly personalized employee/manager relationship in a highly depersonalized world of machines and computers smarter, quicker, and more effective than the people who operate them.

How do you do that?

Super Teams must redesign the design--they've got to break down barriers and physicalize the message: I CARE--YOU MATTER--THIS JOB SHOULD BE FUN.

Case study: "Green lights"

Re: Look what happens when people have fun with their workplace . . .

Jay Chiat, co-founder of the Chiat-Day-Mojo advertising agency, has a simple goal: to be the most creative communications resource in the world. To accomplish this, he's given his team the most creative environment possible to work in.

The pirate flag outside their 50,000 square foot "warehouse office" in Venice, California, is just a tickle before the big smiles inside.

"Main Street." No lobby, no typical reception area, just Main Street--a free-form space complete with vintage autos, an employee art gallery, and a giant silver whale.

Fish Conference Room. Off Main Street is a huge, fish-shaped conference room. In it is a large, oddly shaped table with no "head" and no "foot." This way no one sits in the premier spot. There are no power chairs, either. Everyone's equal.

Electronic Reader Board. This flashes with the motivational thought of the day. The last time we were there it said, "All things are delicately interconnected."

No Paper, Please. Their communications goal: eradicate all paper memos. If you can't say it in person, leave it on my computer.

Stress Management. A basketball hoop is in the center of the space. Use it any time. You can slam-dunk anything. Just make sure it bounces.

Change As a Theme. Everything is constantly changing--clients, the business environment, and us. Employees can change their work stations as often as they need to, and are encouraged to be happy and flexible.

The Bottom Line:

> The firm has gone from zero billing to $1.2 billion in 23 years, and was voted Agency of the Decade by Advertising Age magazine.

In praise of the "green light" environment

Chiat-Day-Mojo's "warehouse offices" prove that workers are conditioned by their environment. Now some might suggest that the CDM team is so successful because they're creative to begin with, and that the lighthearted comfort of their surroundings has nothing to do with the bottom line.

Laurie Coots, VP of Administration, would disagree emphatically.

> *"Our fun environment keeps reinforcing that we're here to enjoy ourselves, open up, make contact with everybody, not be afraid to try new things--and to have a ball working the best way we know how. The space gives us permission to be creative."*

New Breed Workers are probably the most environment-sensitive employees in history. Consider. They come to work, synthesized music blasting in their radio headsets, wearing a psychedelic array of colors and patterns right out of a Fellini dream sequence. They slither into designer space suits for their lunchtime aerobics class, finish work, and go home to watch 182 TV channels scooped out of the air from a special dish that can reach every corner of the world. They eat gourmet microwave dinners in less time than it took to buy them. They fax, VCR, MTV, and mobile-phone away their in-between time.

You could call all that sensory overload, and you might be right. But you still would not be in a position to ignore your workers' way of life.

You must appeal to your employees' senses.

179

The park has got to fit the spirit of the game. You can't pull off the world's most humanized process of employee "participation" and "empowerment" in a space designed for a penitent monk.

Work should be a passion, not an interruption

Redesign for a bright, upbeat, open space that nurtures:

> Informality
> Open access to all levels
> "Lightness" of being

Informality. Dinosaur work spaces were built to intimidate, to hold people in check, to make them conform, to encourage the desire to be average. In short, they were built to do all the things a Light Manager has to erase if he or she is to give the "green light" to workers to excel.

Informality confirms that you want people relaxed and open.

At Winterhur Swiss, a reinsurance company in downtown Manhattan, upper level offices, conference rooms, and reception areas are decked out with warm, homey living room furniture instead of the stuffy, unreal pieces you usually find in the executive suite.

Check out your dentist's waiting room. The modern tooth doctor understands that if you remove the anticipation of fear from the patient, you will have a more satisfied patient. Notice all the funny pictures on the wall, the soothing music, and the comfy couches in the anteroom. Meanwhile, at Ben and Jerry's Ice Cream headquarters in Waterbury, Vermont, there are changing tables for babies in both the women's and men's rest rooms.

"Green light" strategy

Have your team target your biggest environmental eyesore.

Run a contest to get a redesign to "soften the blow."

Make a show of the "make-over."

181

66 Any time you change color, you improve productivity. People first react to newness, then a deeper response to the specific color kicks in. **99**

Carlton Wagner
Wagner Institute of Color
Santa Barbara, California

White promotes precision.

Darks are intimidating.

Grey helps creative people become more artistic.

Pinks speed processes and dexterity tasks such as strokes per minute in word processing.

Browns cause people to talk, open up.

Greens are comfortable and put you at ease.

Sky blue gives a sense of trust and security.

WORKSPACE: "Green Light" Environments

Open access to all levels. Current trends indicate that by the year 2000, about 90% of the work force will be working in an automated office. More people will be interacting with more machines than the most imaginative science fiction writer ever envisioned. With diminishing space a crucial factor, it will be plenty crowded, too. The cubby hole or "rat maze" design will appear to be the more cost-effective choice.

Super Teams seem equally divided on the issue of systems furniture with movable partitions, but they are unanimous in making certain that in whatever systems they choose, two standards apply. First, the partitions must be low enough so a team member can stand and have a direct view of the windows and other team members. Second, senior management must have direct, open access to the team.

Your design must encourage more contact and communications.

The elitist corner office with the closed door does not serve the need of open communications on all levels. It will be sure to die hard, since many upwardly mobile executives see that perk as the ultimate sign of success. But die it must. It does not serve new needs.

"Green light" strategy

Have each Team Member conduct his or her own crucial task need study at his or her work station before you redesign.

Don't impose a design on the Team. Share the architect/designer with your people. Make it "their" design.

Reserve space within each work station for individual "decorator magic."

Hold a contest twice a year for the best "decorator magic" within a work station. It keeps people changing and freshens up your look.

183

" Build the spaces you want your people to be the most creative in. "

Jay Chiat , Co-founder/Chairman of the board
Chiat -Day-Mojo Advertising

WORKSPACE: "Green Light" Environments

"Lightness" of being. Put out the physical signs that clearly announce you are not working in the middle of a Eugene O'Neill tragedy. It can be as simple as providing a yogurt machine in the cafeteria with a sign that says, "Have a swirl on us--enjoy!" (That's what Maui Inter-Continental does for its team.)

Low on funds? Follow the lead of John Smith, CEO of Sports 'A Foot. He gave every one of his store managers a bunch of brushes and a section of paint and asked them to renovate the employee restrooms in the most innovative way their imaginations would allow. Another low-budget master touch: an art show featuring the work of your employees' children. The theme: "My Mommy/Daddy at Work."

Start your lightening up process in the single most effective place to send the rest of the Team that message: *the CEO's office!* Decorate it for communication--not coronation. You want people "off-guard" in your office. That's when you hear the truth. Ditch the personal war trophies; feature the "Team's Accomplishment." Buy a big, comfortable couch. Get out from behind your desk and talk to your team on that couch. In the New Economy, informality is power. Take the silliest fun memento you have at home and transfer it to your office. Put it in plain sight.

"Green light" strategy

Don't design fun--let the team do it. Dramatize your desire to lighten up the environment by picking either the cafeteria or the break rooms; then ask for drawings on how to put some fun in those areas. The ball will roll!

This job should be FUN

Color the park

Let there be color, light, and plenty of LURs (Lighten Up Reminders). Be a makeover freak. Everything can be spruced up. The Napa, California garbage service took big, lumbering trash trucks, painted them white, hung four-by-eight paintings of serene outdoor scenery, and turned them into a magnificent, gleaming, mobile museum. Bravo!

Find a mascot

The Super Team at Multi-Media Corporation dubbed an oversized mannequin of a smiling country bumpkin their "Chairman of the Board Emeritus." They kept it in their conference room to soften all their heavy-duty meetings. Find yours. It will become the centerpiece of much good fun.

Dancing boards

Design your bulletin boards for attention. Lots of color, creative lettering, and fun. It's a cheap way to brighten any space. It's also the only way you'll get people to read what you want them to read.

Name the monster

The Super Team at the Desert   Inn Hotel call their underground service tunnels "Mole City, U.S.A." They take great pride in keeping them clean and shiny. Target your biggest area of discomfort and, if you can't change it, make fun with it. "Mole City" is home to the annual employee art show.

186

WORKSPACE: "Green Light" Environments

Makeover surgical team

Appoint a fun group to suggest colorful "surgery" on your spaces.

Start where it counts the most

Show your team personal care by renovating the personal areas first--restrooms, locker rooms, and cafeteria.

This Job Should Be Fun

The Light Manager's ACTION check-off

☐ 1. Target.

Have your team target every ugly spot you've got for extinction or makeover.

☐ 2. Make an immediate impression.

Start in the "personal" areas first.

188

In the New Reality, Light Managers know . . .

There is a New Breed Worker who craves stimulation and freedom of expression in his or her environment.

They want to feel good about where they are.

You have to work with them to shine the light in every dark corner you have.

APPENDIX A:
A "Quick Buzzthrough" of Great Ideas
Specific "Lighten Up" Programs That Produce Results

" The bottom line of a fun program is that heavy duty people-problems get solved without all the ugly feudin', fussin', and fightin' that makes most work so miserable. "

Betty Moss
Management Engineering, Maui, Hawaii

" History and tradition are what keep teams together, and the great ones always dress up both with fun . . . lots of fun. I've never met a humorless winning team. "

Dick Glander
Consultant, Communications Electronics
Miami, Florida

This Job Should Be Fun

The following "fun" programs have been picked from hundreds
we have studied. We have found them to be the most
immediately effective activities with a bottom-line impact. Try
some.

Inter-department cooperation

Message: Conflict doesn't work. Your department and my
department have got to cooperate now.

"Lemonade committees"

Establish a tradition when one department is in conflict with
another: make lemonade out of the "lemons."

How to: Whenever conflict arises between departments--
overlapping authority, failure to supply materials on time, ignoring
deadlines, or just plain ignorance of the other outfit's operating
needs--call time out, pick a few line personnel from each
department, and have them sit together around a pitcher of
lemonade and work out a cooperative answer.

Continuing company-wide morale boosters

Message: We want you to lighten up and enjoy yourself at work.

"Fun committees"

Odetics, a west coast high-tech firm that makes robots and data
recorders for the space shuttle, has an "official fun committee"
that keeps employees laughing. Their job--come up with
lighthearted gimmicks that break up the tension of their high-
stress work. "Couch potato" contests, Friday sock hops, and
"'50s days" are some of them. And they do their job well.

Odetics has less absenteeism, one of the lowest key- employee turnover rates, and medical costs twenty percent below industry average.

How to: Have each department establish a "fun committee." Their job: come up with one gag, stunt, or mini-show per month. At the year-end Christmas party, have them compete for the "fun committee bit of the year" award.

"Thank God It's Monday" parties

Reverse a tradition. The fun starts at the head of the week instead of at the end: TGIM!

How to: Establish Monday afternoon as party time. Beer, pretzels, and rock 'n roll at the end of the day.

Kids day

Nothing softens an environment more than children on the scene. Let the kids spend a day working alongside Mommy and Daddy. Watch the conflicts disappear and a whole new perspective bloom.

How to: Give each department a day to bring in the kids. (Christmas or Easter vacation is a good time.) Don't do anything special–let them experience what you experience. Make sure the top brass pays a visit.

This Job Should Be Fun

"Pretty baby"

Establish a tradition. Every time a baby is born to a parent within your department, bring the baby in and let Mommy and Daddy show it off. Having a baby around immediately humanizes the work.

How to: Bring in baby and have a picture taken with your team. The parent takes the rest of the day off.

Button day

Once a month, everybody comes in wearing a button with a fun saying (in good taste). Everybody wants to read everybody else's button. This gets strangers together real fast!

How to: Designate a specific day of the month. Let 'em rip.

Aloha Friday

The last day of the work week in Hawaii is designated "Aloha Friday." Employees come to work in relaxed, colorful attire. It is also the most productive day of work for most of the businesses in our fiftieth state.

How to: Start it off department by department so folks get to see tasteful role models. Get some PR mileage out of it. Let your customers know what's going on.

Sunshine reception

Call anyone at Weaver Popcorn Co., in Van Buren, Indiana, and you will hear a bright, cheery, upbeat voice say, "Well, how are you today?" Sure, they have a full-swing employee participation program in gear and sure, they have a Light Manager in Mike Weaver, the CEO. But they also have a sunshine lady as their receptionist, someone who not only greets every visitor and employee with a genuine, high-energy "hello" in person, but maintains that warmth on the phone throughout the day. One employee said, "Her positive attitude is contagious. We all start talking like her on the phone. After a while, everybody is happy."

How to: The quickest way to maintain a positive attitude at work is to change the chemistry on the phone from bland "professionalism" to a high-energy "hello." It sets the tone for everything that follows. Take lots of time to hire your main phone person. Make sure he or she is a genuine, "upbeat person." Encourage and reinforce his or her great phone voice. Name a "Sunshine Award after him or her. Remember, his or her voice is the first impression you customer has of your product.

De-stressing the overstressed

Message: We know you're overworked and under the gun. Relax—take time off on us.

Fun sabbatical

When Andy Maisner was CEO of the American Film Factory, one of the largest post-production facilities in television, he would drop off an envelope on the desk of a particularly stressed employee. The envelope contained tickets to anything from a balloon ride to a trip to Disneyland, from tickets to an afternoon ballgame to a gift certificate for free windsurfing lessons. The employee would have to stop what he or she was doing and fly to the fun. People had a ball managing their stress.

How to: When you see a team member walking on the edge, declare a "Fun Sabbatical." Give the person two tickets to a fun event that day and let him or her go.

"Crazy days"

The Wright and Kimbrough Insurance Agency in Sacramento is very concerned about their team's stress levels. When anyone in the office feels someone, a group, or maybe the entire atmosphere is too uptight, he or she stands up and declares "Crazy Day tomorrow!" They pick a crazy prop or article of clothing--a funny nose, a colorful hat, a silly stuffed animal--and everyone has to come in the next day wearing the fun.

How to: Bring in a funny nose and watch for the arrival of stress. When it hits, whip out your new nose and declare a tradition. Lead the way. (Helpful hint: This would also be a great time to settle all conflicts. It's tough to harbor a grudge against someone when you're wearing an elephant nose.)

Appreciating the night shift

Message: We know you're often overlooked, and we're putting an end to that right now.

The "Midnight Express"

The 630-bed Christian Hospital in St. Louis sends a big expression of appreciation to their night-shift workers by throwing a party in their honor every year and calling it "The Midnight Express."

How to: Stop calling this period of time your "graveyard shift." People who work at night are "Midnight Specials." Get a coffee cart with lots of doughnuts, decorate it, and have one of your top execs wheel it in a few times a year and host an appreciation break. Throw a "Midnight Special" party once a year.

Light Manager's notebook

Lighten up those memos. Humor makes the point . . . and it sticks around longer.

A large Milwaukee company sent all its employees the following note a few days before the opening of the baseball season:

"Any employee desiring to be present at the death or funeral of a relative, please notify the foreman before 10 a.m. the day of the game."

This Job Should Be Fun

Declare a holiday

When Coca-Cola decided to reformulate their number one-selling drink, Pepsi-Cola, their archrival, treated it as a victory. Pepsi declared a one-day holiday for its employees to go home and celebrate. The Pepsi team felt like they were finally king of the mountain.

How to: When you have dramatic evidence that your team is achieving or has achieved the overriding goal, shout it loud and long. Hang out the flag. Declare a holiday!

Surprise visit

Having Dolly Parton, Bob Hope, or Mickey Mantle speak at your convention is fun, but you get a lot more mileage out of presenting celebrities if you bring them to work and introduce them to the line.

How to: Try to start with a local sports celebrity. Contact him or her just to walk around with you and thank folks for the great job they're doing. Don't announce it. Surprise everybody. The surprise will have more emotional impact.

"Number-one customer presses the flesh"

A variation on the theme above--have your number-one customer pay a surprise visit and thank your team for their quality of service.

How to: Call your client and ask. You'd be surprised at how fast they'll accept.

Team appreciation day

Fan appreciation day at the ballpark is usually the biggest promotion of the year for the local team--and the best attended.

It is filled with a colorful array of free gifts and all manner of other bells and whistles saluting the support from the best. People love to be appreciated in a spectacular way. Do it for your work team.

How to: You can't go far enough overboard on this one. Pull out as many stops as you can. Start with breakfast and lunch on the CEO. Have all the managers doing the serving. Strolling violins, a jazz combo, cheerleaders, big prize giveaways, and auctioning off the CEO's parking stall are all swell.

G.L. Anderson, the President of Physio-Control Corporation in Redmond, Washington, announces team appreciation day with a full scale marching band strutting their stuff through the halls and offices at 7:15 a.m.

Sending the message of cooperation to the non-cooperative types

Message: We recognize and reward cooperation as the most important leadership trait in tough times.

Aloha dinners

Aloha dinners are a powerful and gentle way to draw everybody's attention to the fact that cooperation is the only way we win around here. Originally devised by nurses fed up with being treated like slaves by "Dr. Frankenstein," this program can be used by any organization. It's simple. Twice a year you hold a "Hawaiian Luau" with all the colorful decorations and music. The sponsoring department asks each of its members to invite, as his or her guest, one person from another area who has shown "great team spirit and cooperation." After several dinners have passed and you find you haven't been invited, the message comes through loud and clear--start cooperating.

This Job Should Be Fun

How to: Hold these gatherings as many times a year as necessary. Designate one department or group as sponsor. Send invitations to the guests. At the dinner, have the sponsor introduce his or her guest and say a few words about his or her outstanding cooperation. At the end of the year, have each department choose their "Teammate of the Year" from another area.
Remember: Aloha means more than "hello" and "goodbye"; it means you have a genuine caring spirit.

"Write your own ticket"

Along with their "Friday afternoon office parties" and a dozen other colorful stress busters, Apple Computer asks their engineering and marketing folks to write their own job descriptions. It gives people lots of flexibility and the ability to improve their focus. It's controlling one's own life, and that's fun.

How to: Let the team members write out their job descriptions first. They'll be a lot more demanding of themselves than you would have been. They'll give themselves plenty of responsibility. Fine. Applaud that. Then have them sit down with their managers and work out the kinks. Give them free reign to update the description as needed.

Reaching goals should be fun

Message: Setting and reaching goals is what life at work is all about. Let's keep it light.

Target day

Some teams spend a good deal of time analyzing the obstacles to be overcome, then set simple goals and go out and play the game with gusto. The game plan is announced and agreed upon the same day. Everyone is charged at the same time. That simultaneous emotion is the superheat that drives most teams to victory. You can call it "momentum" or 'being charged up" or

"delicatessen." It doesn't matter what you call it. It works.

How to: Distribute large targets to every department. Make sure the bullseye is large enough to write three top goals on. Have team members hang the targets up. When *every* department has reached the appointed goals, celebrate in a big way. Put a large "dunk tank" in the parking lot, stick the CEO inside in front of a large target, and let everyone have one shot.

Homecoming

Once a year colleges and universities celebrate "Homecoming Day," a time to enjoy being a team. Tailgate parties, upbeat music, costumes, marching bands, special recognition, and lots of good-natured "blarney." A good time to reward your team for setting and reaching goals.

How to: Establish a Homecoming tradition; every fall, recognize teams (departments) who have set and reached goals. Make sure *every* team is recognized, and announce each one's most significant achievement. The team with the highest percentage of goals attained wins the big prize (tickets to the big game, for instance). Hold the affair in an outdoor setting. Be sure to pick a Homecoming King and Queen--and feature a skit from a "Fun Committee."

We're always winning at something

Message: We want you to be excited about winning. And everybody has the opportunity to win at something.

Frequent traveler program

By far the most enthusiastically received notion in the airline industry has been the frequent traveler program. Everybody loves to play a game and win a prize. You fly and you get points. You stay at a certain hotel and you get points. You rent a certain car and you get points. There are many ways to win, and often many different prizes available. Use the same strategy to keep your team motivated about winning.

How to: Pick things anybody can win at: attendance and safety. Make it a *team* competition, not an individual achievement. Run it for a short time, no longer than three to five months. Any longer than that and you lose interest. Display progress on a giant scoreboard, the way the Sands Hotel in Las Vegas did. They put the thing in the employee parking lot so everybody was "reminded" all the time.

(Helpful hint: Make the prizes exciting. Travel is always desirable, but "shopping sprees" are now producing the highest emotional response among line workers. Let them loose in a supermarket; they get to take everything they can pile into a shopping basket in, say, twenty minutes. The key is to get an emotional buy-in *before* the contest begins, and the "shopping spree" idea can certainly get the juices flowing.)

Bring Mohammed to the foot of the mountain

Boards of Directors have a terrible habit of perpetuating their own stereotype: a bunch of elitists in overpriced silk suits and diamond pinky rings sitting in a royal chamber making decisions that ignore the peasants and fill their own pockets. The fact is, the Board is at once the most important and the most remote part of your team's future. Posting the minutes from the most recent Board meeting on the company bulletin board is a requirement. Unfortunately, it does nothing to prove you really care about "opening up communications." Change the setting!

How to: Hold the next Board Meeting where it will do the most good: on the line, in a real, live working space. Bring your Board out from behind their veil of mystery. Expose them to the heart and soul of your operation. Hold the meeting in the cafeteria, in the boiler room, in the gym, on the lawn, or in the locker room. Expose them to the people who produce your profit: the line.

Take a ride on the Starship Boobyprize

That's what Stanley F. Hupfield, CEO of the Baptist Medical Center in Oklahoma City, calls the head table at the employee awards dinner. He wears a skinhead wig and a tight body suit–his best effort at an impersonation of Star Trek's Captain Jean-Luc Picard. And he's not alone. All his managers are in equally outrageous attire, dressed as other famous trekkies. The point? To remind people of "the right kind of attitude."

How to: Raid your closet, use a little imagination, and don't be afraid to let people know you don't take yourself seriously *all* the time.

Make recognizing achievement fun

Do away with boring awards banquets–same old chicken, same old brass plaques, same old speeches. Really pump up the troops for the next quarter!

How to: Start by changing the name of your award. "Employee of the Month" has become a cliche. How about "Most Valuable Player"? Or "Mover and Shaker Club Inductee"? Or "Rocky Award Recipient?"

You might also try a new twist on the old theme parties. Who could turn down a Mardi Gras Night invitation? Or one to an Oscar Night or Back to the Future party?

Potpourri: Keeping perspective

Following are some more general ideas on how to make it easier to lighten up at work. Their main goal is to help *you*, the manager, keep on an even keel.

Make fun of yourself--even if you're no Whoopi Goldberg

How? Simple. In the middle of a tense situation, declare your fallibility out loud. Let your folks know you know they know you're not perfect. Start it with, "There I go again . . ."

What's your fault? Not listening? Growling? Not keeping everybody informed? Following the Ebenezer Scrooge school of management? Whatever it is, pop it in the slot. "There I go again, doing my Attila the Hun impersonation--demanding instead of asking."

Take time out in the middle of your winter of discontent to announce your fallibility. Doing so sends the most reassuring signal of all to those around you: *I am a human being! I apologize for being such a pain in the rump!*

Cruise and schmooze

Spend the first fifteen minutes of the day cruising the front line, chewing the fat about anything *except* work. Ask questions about the things people are proud about: kids, spouse, going back to school, annoying in-laws who finally got tossed in the slammer, whatever. People lighten up when you ask them about the things *they* love. So ask.

Give the problem of the day a fun name

Don't curse it--cuddle it. The third-quarter budget meeting becomes "Nightmare on Elm Street Part III." Rename all monsters.

Caption the cartoon

Bring in a cartoon. Cut off the caption. Write your own--to make fun of *you.*

Trash party

Call "Time out." Then take a five-minute drill--everybody has to throw out paperwork, clean out files, straighten up desks, etc.

Baby face

Bring in the silliest baby picture of you. Write two words under it: "Lighten up." Look at it when you feel they ought to name a freeway after you.

Send yourself a bouquet

Send yourself a bouquet of flowers. Write yourself a note: "Remember to smell the flowers."

Cookie monster

Come in early to drop off a cookie (or a carnation, or a chocolate) on each team member's desk. No note. No announcement. Just do it. They'll get the message.

"What if" huddle

Call "Time out." Pick a problem, gather a few people, and start. Ask, "What if we did this a different way?" Don't debate; ask for ideas. Be silly if necessary. Einstein made a point of being silly to help boost his productivity. (Ever see the poster of him sticking his tongue out at the photographer?)

This Job Should Be Fun

Change places

For one hour on Friday, change places with another person in your department.

Take the B-25 approach to personalizing equipment

In World War II, B-25 bomber pilots lumbered into deadly combat with large cartoon insignias emblazoned on their fuselage: "The Ruptured Duck," "Big Mama Rosie," and so on. Do the same with all the machinery you have to deal with. Make them friends.

Ten-second revival meeting

Once a day, stop and give yourself a fabulous pep talk. List in rapid succession all the great things about you: "I'm a great dancer . . . my butcher thinks I'm a doll . . . I don't sweat much . . ."

Smile for no reason at all

It's still the simplest, most immediate way to change your attitude from minus to plus.

Forgive and forget

On the way home, forgive yourself for screwing up, being a boob, and occasionally mistaking the image in the mirror for the Divinity.

High-five it

Everybody wants instant gratification these days. So give in. When good things happen, stop and give a high five--you know, the hand-slapping congratulatory ritual the athletes use. Customize your own department's high five. (The Oakland A's knock forearms.) This type of thing brings emotion to the workplace and lets people know it's okay to show emotion.

Go to cassette college

Never, never, never listen to the radio on the way to work. It's too dangerous. Radios are out to get you. Radios spew out all sorts of harsh, outlook-lowering sounds. Radios specialize in disastrous news that is incapable of inspiring. Invest in positive learning tapes. Start your day with an earful of hope--not Def Leppard or bulletins about the latest tragedy.

Display I.N.T.I.

Write the words "It's not *that* important" on your phone, computer, or desk clock. When the vultures start gathering, look at it. Feel your pulse. If it seems to be present, and if you're still breathing, you're fine. *Breathing* is important. The rest is all second team.

Get a piranha-in-the-box

Place a small black box on your desk (or in a conspicuous spot). When the "Worry Bug" comes prowling, open the box. Shout your fear. Close the box. The invisible piranha-in-the-box will handle all your Worry Bugs.

Eight steps to making it all work

Of the 2,700 managers we interviewed for this book, 741 were committed by temperament or conscious choice to send the *I Care--You Matter--This Job Should Be Fun* message to their teams. Apart from this attitude, they had very little else in common.

They came in all shapes, sizes, colors, personality types, and salary ranges. We were able, however, to clearly identify eight positive actions used by all of them to "lighten up" their environment.

One: Refuse to take any news tragically. Workers take their attitudinal cues from the front office. The most powerful leadership tool is to radiate hope in tough times--to refuse to catch the "woe is me" bug. It's the most contagious disease there is in any organization. Herman Cain, CEO of the Godfather Pizza chain, faces all calamities with his staff with the same words: "Okay, what good can we learn from this . . . and let's do it." When one of their high-volume stores in Seattle burned to the ground, Herman asked his question and the staff responded, "We can remodel it and make it better than before." They did--and volume has increased.

Two: Erase all negative criticism. The most destructive communication there is to a team fabric is negative criticism--always pointing the finger of blame, bawling folks out for being less than archangels in their work. That's the best way to destroy self-esteem and make enemies for life. Federal Express, for one, doesn't allow anybody to talk down to anybody else, period. If you persist in such activities, you're history. So--try to attack behavior, not people. Don't say, "Johnson, stop giving the shipping department a hard time." Say, "Johnson, we need stronger cooperation between you and shipping. How can we do that?"

Three: Specific thank you's. Get out of the habit of giving people general praise. Things like "Nice job," "Thanks for the good work," and "You're all doing great," are dismissed by the New Breed Worker as insincere. When you cite the behavior you're rewarding, the recipient knows you mean it. Say, "Thanks, Helen, for staying overtime to finish that sales report."

Four: Happy hello in the a.m. The first half-hour at work is the most critical. That's when your conscious mind sets its mood for the rest of the day. Greet everybody in that time frame with a big, hearty, "Good morning." It has the power to change the traditional early-morning blahs into a bright beginning. Next time you're at a five-start hotel, watch how many of the staff go out of their way to greet guests in the morning. It's part of service excellence training.

Five: Overcome seriosa nervosa. Well over seventy percent of the managers in our fun survey were suffering from this curable disease--taking yourself too damn seriously. Managers who exhibit the symptoms of this malady send the most unproductive message possible to their team: "We're in the middle of a swamp and things aren't going to get any better." The most therapeutic use of humor at work is to direct it against *self!*

Six: Make merry on the phone. The quickest way to change the chemistry of an organization is to change the way people talk on the phone. Most conversations at work are about negative things, and are delivered in a negative emotional voice. Call the South Carolina Board of Health and you'll get a cheery "Good morning--and how are ya?" Answer your phone with high positive energy. It puts you in charge, and puts the conversation on a positive footing.

Seven: Color your corner. Light Managers know formality destroys honest communications. Decorate your office for informal openness. You want people loose, off-guard, so you can hear the truth. Ditch the trophy cases and the Palace of Versailles crystal accessories, and design for comfort. Super Hotel executive Bill Friedman always lines his office with his famous Mickey Mouse dolls--unless, of course, there's room for his two pinball machines. "You'd be surprised," says Bill, "how quickly visitors loosen up and tell me the real scoop."

This Job Should Be Fun

Eight: Look for the right way, not your way. President Mike Weaver of Weaver Popcorn in Indiana always walks the production line and asks folks for their best suggestion to overcome a particular problem. He even goes a step further and encourages everybody to question his judgment--any time, any place. "I want to hear if there's a better way," he says. One of his truck drivers told us, "It really makes it fun when you know the boss wants you to tell him if he screwed up." Don't debate. Just listen.

APPENDIX B:
Are You a Light Manager?

Are You a Light Manager?

"I CARE. YOU MATTER. THIS JOB SHOULD BE FUN."

How effectively are you sending the message? Take the following test and find out.

The only way to improve staff performance is to change the messages you are sending to your team. You have to determine first just what messages you are now sending, second, what ares need improving, and third, how you'll commit to action.

Directions: Write down the number that best describes your present behavior in relation to the following statements.

Always: 5
Usually: 4
Fairly Often: 3
Occasionally: 2
Rarely: 1
Never: 0

Then add up your total points after each category and enter them under "My Score" at the end of each section.

PRIMARY FUNCTION

My team knows I believe in sharing power with the line. _____

Everyone working for me knows exactly what results are expected of them. _____

An achievement graph is posted to show the entire department how well they're doing. _____

My praise is specific. _____

Perfect score: 20   My score:

This Job Should Be Fun

COMMUNICATIONS

I level with my team (tell them the truth). _____

Everyone knows our overriding goal. _____

My door is always open. _____

I daily ask the question, "Is there anything I can help you with?" _____

I get new information out quickly. _____

When I describe a complicated procedure, I break it down to more easily understood steps. _____

I talk slow enough for everyone to understand me. _____

I speak directly to my people rather than write memos. _____

If I do hold a meeting, it's a free, open exchange. _____

When delivering bad news, I end on a hopeful note. _____

I avoid giving orders. I say, "Would you please . . ." _____

When asking someone to do something new, I explain why. _____

Perfect score: 60   My score:

LEADERSHIP

I resolve all conflict in the boo-boo stage. _____

My team knows I have a passion to achieve one overriding goal. _____

I criticize the behavior, not the person. _____

I spend fifty percent of my time on the line with my staff. _____

I solve problems "on the spot." _____

I allow people to question my methods. _____

My people know I'm on call twenty-four hours a day. _____

My personal grooming is a model for the staff. _____

I praise in public, correct in private. _____

I criticize to help, not to punish. _____

I take time to understand my staff's point of view. _____

I make the rounds of our workspaces every day. _____

My department is capable of running effectively without me around. _____

I am willing to terminate an employee who, after generous amounts of training, coaching, and patience, simply doesn't measure up. _____

Perfect score: 65   My score:

LISTENING

I make eye contact with people I speak to. _____

When someone complains to me, I take notes. _____

I consider all news from the front line important. _____

I ask simple questions. _____

I don't interrupt answers. _____

My staff knows I want to listen to their concerns. _____

This Job Should Be Fun

I ask lots of questions. _____

I'm genuinely interested in what people have to tell me. _____

I'm patient with slow people. _____

I am careful not to criticize when I do not have all the facts. _____

Perfect score: 50   My score:

MOTIVATING

I ask everybody to contribute to prioritizing the goals in our department. _____

I ask everybody to contribute to writing our operating standards and procedures. _____

I ask all employees what they want from their job. _____

I allow employees to evaluate themselves. _____

I help identify obstacles in personal improvement plans. _____

I am a role for the idea of enthusiasm for one's work. _____

Everyone knows the most urgent problem to solve in our department. _____

I ask for advice. _____

I say "thank you" for a job well done. _____

I don't hesitate to tell people when their performance is not acceptable. _____

Are You a Light Manager?

I know what everybody's "feel good" button is. _____

Perfect score: 55   My score:

ATTITUDE

I enthusiastically greet every staff member in the morning. _____

I am a role model for the kind of attitude I want my staff to show the customer/client. _____

I approach all negative situations with a smile. _____

My temper is controlled. _____

I have an open, approachable manner. _____

I ask for people's opinions before I change anything. _____

I accentuate the positive. _____

It's obvious I want my staff to be the best. _____

Perfect score: 40   My score:

TRAINING

There is an ongoing training plan in my department. _____

Every veteran has been told he or she is a trainer. _____

I personally help train every new hire. _____

Everyone is evaluated every ninety days. _____

My people are trained to solve problems at their level. _____

This Job Should Be Fun

Every time I see an improper procedure, I make a mental note to retrain that person. _____

There are simple written standards of excellence in our department. _____

Perfect score: 35   My score:

DELEGATING
(Giving people authority to do things on their own)

When I delegate a job, the person knows what I expect because I tell them clearly. _____

I give credit to those who do the job. _____

I support people in getting their work done. _____

When people present me with a problem, I ask, "What would you do to solve it?" _____

I allow people to do the job their way. _____

My front line knows they have the authority to solve problems. _____

I praise independent behavior. _____

Perfect score: 35   My score:

Are You a Light Manager?

PERSONAL CARING

I know at least three personal things about each worker's family. _____

I ask about each worker's family. _____

I know each worker's biggest source of personal pride. _____

I have invited each staff member's family to visit the workspace. _____

I recognize when someone is going through tough times at home. _____

My staff's lavatory and locker facilities are spotless. _____

I follow through on all promises. _____

Perfect score: 35   My score:

FUN

I refuse to take any news tragically. _____

Our team has a bright, cheery, colorful workspace. _____

We have "fun" morale booster events. _____

We vigorously celebrate birthdays. _____

I spring "fun" surprises on our team. _____

I celebrate our victories. _____

I post our victories. _____

Are You a Light Manager?

We have a department incentive program. _____

I make fun of myself in front of the staff. _____

I allow my team to have fun. _____

I call staff by their first names. _____

Perfect score: 55   My score:

RATE YOURSELF

If your score is between:

420-455 (Congratulations! Welcome to the ranks of Light Managers.)

380-419 (You're close. Target improvement.)

365-379 (You're within striking distance. Target lots of improvement.)

Below 365 (You could be getting much more effort from your team with a systematized approach to care.)

HOW TO TARGET IMPROVEMENT

Identify ten categories of a Light Manager's responsibility where you scored a three or less. Put a large circle around the description of the quality. These areas need work.

COMMIT TO ACTION

You have effectively identified your areas of needed improvement. Start now. Pick *one* of your circled areas in each category and write it below on the appropriate line.

PRIMARY FUNCTION
_____

COMMUNICATIONS
_____

LEADERSHIP
_____

LISTENING
_____

MOTIVATING
_____

ATTITUDE
_____

TRAINING
_____

DELEGATING
_____

PERSONAL CARING
_____

FUN
_____

This Job Should Be Fun

Each day, pick one area and start a positive action toward making it happen.

Lighten up and win!

APPENDIX C:
Setting Up M-I-B Teams

The keys to M-I-B (Make-It-Better) success are *informality* and *flexibility*. Nothing is written in concrete. Structure the teams to fit your interests.

Starting the M-I-B ball rolling

Step one. Announce at your department meeting that *we* need volunteers to form an M-I-B team (usually no fewer than four , no more than nine). The first to volunteer from the first meeting are selected. They will conduct the business--however, *anyone* from the department can attend as guests. M-I-B is totally democratic and belongs to every member of the department who wishes to participate.

Step two. Appoint the most senior member of the volunteer group to chair. This job will rotate every meeting to the next most senior member present. Set a meeting date. Post it.

Announce that subsequent M-I-B meetings will be run by the people who originally volunteered. If there are not enough people available to fill the quota, post a notice and ask for volunteers. The key is to keep the membership rotating among new people, giving everybody a chance to participate. (Larger organizations sometimes opt for electing members on a limited-time basis--usually three months.) Electing member should only be tried after the "open rotation system" has failed. Employees should be given the opportunity to make the process work; try to pump as much fresh blood into the system as possible.

Step three. A staff member from the training department should act as facilitator for the first meeting and then bow out. Make it clear that *management will not sit in on these meetings*, that M-I-B is a staff program. M-I-B Teams may, however, invite managers and other guests from time to time.

Step four. Conduct the meeting. Fill in report forms and deliver them to the appropriate manager for action.

This Job Should Be Fun

Step five. No later than forty-eight hours after receiving the M-I-B report, the manager posts his or her response. The manager also sends a copy to his or her immediate superior.

Step six. If the manager fails to respond in the assigned time, the next higher authority gently but firmly reminds him or her that *participative management will only work if WE maintain passion for immediate response to staff needs.* (If the manager fails a second time to respond on time, some form of disciplinary action must be instituted.) Some organizations have made the manager's response time a contest, posting the scores of managers who have met or responded sooner than required. Putting this information in the newsletter box score also keeps managers on their toes.

Showing passion and consistent commitment to responding quickly to staff needs is the most effective force to improve and increase productivity.

The format

Keep it light, upbeat, and focused on the issues. The most successful M-I-B chairpersons have learned to say, "Let's handle the most urgent matters first."

Start on time. Announce the precise time for quitting, as well. Put everyone on notice that idle chatter wastes valuable time.

Read the guidelines. "We're here for one reason and one reason only--to make it better for all of us. We must make it easier for us to enjoy what we do, and we must remove whatever obstacles stand in the way. We need only positive solutions to problems. We ask you not to bring up any negative griping, politicking, or badmouthing of others. We're here to find new ways to cooperate. Okay; let's make it better."

Ask for the most urgent suggestions. The categories to consider are: Open Communications; Improving Quality of Customer Service; Cost Savings; Staff Morale; Physical Environment; New Ideas; and (if time permits) Comments

Explain the problems. After a problem is brought up, ask everyone to explain *why* it's a problem.

Ask for solutions. After a reasonable amount of time, ask, "Does everyone understand the problem?" When they do, ask for solutions, vote to determine the best one (majority rules!), and write the winner down on your report sheet.

Announce the next meeting time. At the conclusion of the meeting, announce the next meeting time, post it, and talk it up with your fellow workers.

How to get what you want from management (a guide for M-I-B participants)

Stop "us vs. them" thinking. Only cooperation will get you what you want.

Ask for small things. See the request as part of the whole. Patch one hole before you ask for a new roof.

Explain why your suggestion will improve performance and reduce costs in the long run.

Don't offer opinions. Offer solutions.

In big matters, suggest a trial run on a small scale, with the M-I-B Team evaluating the results within a reasonable amount of time.

Always forward a solution to *improve the quality of service.*

Always forward a solution on *cost savings* (simplifying work).

Don't ask for someone else to study a problem in your area; suggest that your M-I-B Team take responsibility for analysis.

This Job Should Be Fun

Invite your manager to sit in (silently) on one of your meetings as a guest as a gesture of cooperation and good faith.

Ask your manager to allow one of your team members to sit in on one of the managers' M-I-B Team Meetings.

Under "Comments," find something to say "thank you" for.

Hints for the chairperson: Making M-I-B work during the meeting

Time. Stay on time! Forty-five minutes--no longer. Keeping to a strict time limit disciplines your team to focus on issues, eliminate meaningless chatter, and get to solutions. If you haven't finished in forty-five minutes, end the meeting anyway! It will send a strong message: "We're here to concentrate on solutions." (Another tip: *announce how much time is left every fifteen minutes.*)

Coaching the agenda. Stick to the six categories in order. If there is no interest in one, quickly move to the next. Don't linger. Repeat the agreed-upon solution before writing it down. Keep an eye on the clock; if the team is spending a great deal of time on one issue, let them know you may not get to other areas. Finally, remember that, in all matters, *majority rules.* If everyone agrees to spend the most amount of time on one issue, so be it. When in doubt, call for a quick vote.

Keeping the team on track. Keep discussions to a bare minimum. Ask, "Does everyone understand the problem?" When they all do, ask for solutions, vote on it, and write it down. *Important: Do not tolerate any form of personal attack by any party!* Say, "I think it's important to remember we'll all get much more out of this if we attack behavior, not people. How can we state this problem in terms of the issue (what the person is doing) and not the personality?"

SAMPLE M-I-B TEAM REPORT

Dept. (Unit): _____
Date: _____
TOS: _____
Response Due: _____

MAKE-IT-BETTER TEAM REPORT

SOLUTIONS

Open Communications:

1. Problem: _____
    Solution: _____
    _____
    MR: _____
    _____

2. Problem: _____
    Solution: _____
    _____
    MR: _____
    _____

Improving Quality of Customer Service:

1. Problem: _____
    Solution: _____
    _____
    MR: _____
    _____

2. Problem: _____
    Solution: _____
    _____
    MR: _____
    _____

Cost Savings (Simplifying Work):

1. Problem: _____
    Solution: _____
    _____
    MR: _____
    _____

2. Problem: _____
    Solution: _____
    _____
    MR: _____
    _____

Key
TOS = Time of Submission
MR = Manager's Response

Staff Morale:

1. Problem: _____
    Solution: _____
    _____
    MR: _____
    _____

2. Problem: _____
    Solution: _____
    _____
    MR: _____
    _____

Physical Environment:

1. Problem: _____
    Solution: _____
    _____
    MR: _____
    _____

2. Problem: _____
    Solution: _____
    _____
    MR: _____
    _____

New Ideas (Products, services, making work fun):

1. Problem: _____
    Solution: _____
    _____
    MR: _____
    _____

2. Problem: _____
    Solution: _____
    _____
    MR: _____
    _____

COMMENTS: _____
_____
_____
_____

MR posted (Date) _____

Manager's Signature _____

Making it work after the meeting: Hints for the manager's response

Response time. Develop a passion for responding quickly. Your staff ultimately make up their minds on your real degree of caring by how quickly you respond to their needs and by what language you use in stating your position. Post your reply *before* the forty-eight hour deadline if at all possible. The quicker you respond to their needs, the quicker they will respond to yours and those of the customer. Create urgency. It's contagious. (Also important: apologize if you're tardy!)

How you respond

Don't say "no." And keep the writing informal.

Leave the door of hope open. You will not be able to implement many of the solutions; just make sure your rejections are clothed in positive language. The quickest way to kill Participative Management is with a consistent string of cold "no's." Below are some examples of positive responses.

"Very sound idea. No budget at this time, but if you folks could come up with some cost-saving ways to start the ball rolling, we could jump into this immediately."

"Not too clear how this would work. Please re-think a step-by-step process and maybe we could find a way to get it done."

"Can't see how this would take priority over other goals, but am willing to be convinced."

Kill the "I"! Use the language of cooperation: "WE." When you see possibilities, ask for more information. Track yourself. Copy your responses. Compare them often. What real messages are you sending your folks, positive or negative?

This Job Should Be Fun

Share your responsibility. Occasionally give your M-I-B Team a management project you might otherwise keep for yourself. This program needs dramatic evidence to *prove you care.*

Give specific pats on the back. Let your team know personally and in writing (and in front of the entire department when possible) when a specific action led to positive results. General praise is usually perceived as disingenuous. *Specific praise motivates.*

Making M-I-B Teams work from start to finish

Track the results. The team loses interest in any feedback system if there aren't some dramatic examples illustrating that their input was implemented. Keep department-by-department results of all suggestions made and what percentage of them have been implemented. Be particularly careful to highlight *quality improvement* and *cost savings.*

Target ".200 hitters" for assistance. Teams showing little progress should be visited and trained by successful peer group M-I-B members.

Establish an M-I-B Team Council: Have two members from each M-I-B Team meet with two members from all the other department M-I-Bs and find solutions for problems that cross department lines. Send their solutions directly to the CEO.

Rename your in-house publication! Get "M-I-B" in the title, or format a large section devoted to M-I-B progress. Display results in a newsletter boxscore. The staff has got to see progress to reinforce support for the program.

Make superstars of successful teams! Point to your role models. Sing their praises loud and often. After a reasonable shakedown period (say, six months), ask all teams to suggest an incentive program for top M-I-B Teams.

Keep the CEO involved--and very visible--in the program. Pick key M-I-B Teams and have the CEO pay guest visits as a silent observer. This is a very strong reinforcement the whole staff will talk about for some time to come.

Make it fun! Make all your fun competition (bowling leagues, picnic games, special events) between M-I-B Teams, not just departments. Encourage one M-I-B Team to challenge another to match their record of accomplishment--but keep it light!

The most frequently asked questions about M-I-B

We've got too many people in our division to be served by only one M-I-B Team. What do we do?

Form an M-I-B Team for every common area of interest within the division. For instance, the Maintenance Division may need M-I-Bs for Grounds, Interior Systems, Power Plant, and Records.

What do you do when some people seem to be monopolizing the voting membership of every meeting?

Report it to the training department or human resources department, whichever is designated to supervise the overall administration of M-I-B.

The trainer will make it known to that department that M-I-B is set up to give everybody a chance at being a delegate. He or she will also send the message that new members have to be served first.

This Job Should Be Fun

What do you do if you don't have a quorum?

Reschedule and start talking it up. M-I-B is your best shot at getting changes made. Support it or fall behind!

Our manager keeps attending and trying to run things. What do we do?

Gently but affirmatively remind him or her that managers may only attend when they are invited by the team. If that doesn't work, call the training or human resources department and let them pass along the word.

Do we have to stick to the six categories you've outlined?

No! If there is a category of particular importance to your department, write it in. It's your team, and it's your life at work you're making better. Do what's necessary.

How do we stop all the arguing and useless debating?

Ask the training or human resources department to send a facilitator to show people how to present the problem clearly, explain it in a positive framework, and then vote on the best solution. Do all your debating before the meeting.

Can we meet more than once a month?

Yes! Meet as often as your needs demand.

Can we go beyond the allotted time?

No. Call another meeting.

Other teams seem to be getting more done than us. How do we get more of what we want?

Invite a member from those successful teams to your meeting and find out. It's your ballgame. Use all the players you have to win.

APPENDIX D:
Light Manager's Guide to Hot Legal Issues

Please note:

The following pages outline only a few of the hot issues. The law varies greatly from state to state, so consult your attorney where in doubt.

Hot issue: Sexual harassment

Unlawful behavior: Sexual advances made as a condition for favorable treatment; or hostile environment created by sexual comments and/or treatment.

Dinosaur attitude: Sexist jokes, soliciting sexual favors, dates, touching; treating work as if it were a singles club or locker room.

Light Manager's response: Creates a positive, healthy work environment, free of sexual comments, behavior, innuendoes; treats all workers as equal associates.

Hot issue: Termination

Unlawful behavior: Terminating employees contrary to the terms of company policy, manual, contract, or public policy. (Oral and written agreements are to be regarded as equally important.)

Dinosaur attitude: Firing without "just cause"; failing to objectively investigate employee problems. Acting arbitrarily; disregarding company procedures and/or ignoring importance of treating all employees fairly.

Light Manager's response: Fires employees only as a last resort and only for "just cause." Listens, communicates, and does everything possible to nip employee problems in the bud.

Hot issue: Equal opportunity

Unlawful behavior: Discrimination; refusing to hire qualified applicants as a result of racial, sexual, or other prejudice; treating employees differently (directly or indirectly) because of person's race, color, religion, national origin, gender, or sexual preference. (Includes pregnant women, homosexuals, and AIDS victims.)

Dinosaur attitude: Showing favoritism; acting out his or her own prejudices; treating employees unfairly. (Subtle behavior is as bad as overt discrimination.)

Light Manager's response: Focuses only on employee's qualifications and is thoroughly trained in the "language" of nondiscrimination.

Hot issue: Drug testing

Unlawful behavior: While pre-hiring drug testing is allowed in private industry, post-hire testing must be guaranteed to be "random" in nature *or* to be the result of a reasonable suspicion.

Dinosaur attitude: Falsely claiming to have post-hiring drug testing program that is scientifically random--and that is not based on personal selection or unreasonable suspicion of one single employee.

Light Manager's response: Carefully restricts, monitors, and controls drug testing policy and practice, guaranteeing randomness or limiting specific testing to cases where safety is an issue. Keeps on top of all the legal hot spots.

Hot issue: Smoking

Unlawful behavior: Ignoring requests of non-smokers for a smoke-free work environment or area.

Dinosaur attitude: Failing to adopt a policy to satisfy smokers and non-smokers.

Light Manager's response: Makes every reasonable accommodation for a smoke-free environment and designates certain public areas as non-smoking.

Hot issue: Toxic substances

Unlawful behavior: Failure to give notification/information on each and every toxic substance found in the workplace.

Dinosaur attitude: "What they don't know won't hurt them."

Light Manager's response: Prepares and makes readily available full information on hazardous substances at work. Maintains file for all to review and provides employee education on toxants.

Hot issue: Illegal aliens

Unlawful behavior: Knowingly or unknowingly hiring someone who is an illegal alien.

Dinosaur attitude: Failing to verify whether a prospective employee is an unauthorized alien (someone without papers to work in the U.S.).

Light Manager's response: Sets record-keeping procedures and practices for screening aliens.

Hot issue: Union activities

Unlawful behavior: Preventing, thwarting, or firing workers who try to unionize.

Dinosaur attitude: Trying every possible means to ignore/sabotage workers who desire to unionize.

Light Manager's response: Goes out of his or her way to identify the grievance causing the problems, and actively tries to work it out with employees.

Hot issue: Whistleblowing/retaliation

Unlawful behavior: Threatening or firing employees who attempt to "turn the company in" for wrongdoing.

Dinosaur attitude: Maintaining a secretive, distrustful, noncommunicative atmosphere about serious corporate problems.

Light Manager's response: Keeps everything out in the open; encourages and challengers the worker to challenge the company about its regulations and/or product integrity.

APPENDIX E:
Blank Evaluation Forms

The forms on the following pages are the best evaluation forms we've yet seen. They are reproduced with the kind permission of Rick Ralston at Crazy Shirts in the fair state of Hawaii.

EMPLOYEE EVALUATION OF SUPERVISOR

Name of Supervisor:_____ Title:_____

Period of Evaluation:_____ to _____

Instructions to the Evaluator: Completion of this form is voluntary – you do not have to evaluate your supervisor if you prefer not to. Your signature at the end is also optional. The purpose is to help supervisors improve their management skills by identifying strengths as well as areas where improvement is desirable.

Do not let your personal feelings affect your rating – rate only on performance, not on personality. Base your evaluation on the typical performance for the entire period not on isolated instances which are not typical. You should be able to support your rating with comments and examples that are as specific and as factual as possible.

When you are finished, return the completed form to the Human Resources Department. It will be sent to your supervisor's immediate supervisor. Your supervisor will **not** see your comments.

	Excellent	Good	Fair	Poor
Sets a good example for others	_____	_____	_____	_____
Creates a positive work environment	_____	_____	_____	_____
Motivates employees to do their best	_____	_____	_____	_____
Gives clear directions/communicates well	_____	_____	_____	_____
Is a good listener	_____	_____	_____	_____
Plans and organizes department functions	_____	_____	_____	_____
Is generally fair in decision making	_____	_____	_____	_____
Gives regular feedback on performance	_____	_____	_____	_____
Provides adequate support to complete tasks	_____	_____	_____	_____
Is willing to consider new ideas/suggestions	_____	_____	_____	_____
Is empathetic to employees' concerns	_____	_____	_____	_____
Acts professionally/creates positive image	_____	_____	_____	_____

Areas of greatest strength:

Areas where improvement is desirable:

General Comments:

_____   _____
Evaluator's Signature (optional)   Date

EMPLOYEE EVALUATION OF SUPERVISOR

Name of Supervisor:_____ Title:_____
Period of Evaluation:_____ to _____

<u>Instructions to the Evaluator</u>: Completion of this form is voluntary - you do not have to
evaluate your supervisor if you prefer not to. Your signature at the end is also
optional. The purpose is to help supervisors improve their management skills by
identifying strengths as well as areas where improvement is desirable.

Do not let your personal feelings affect your rating - rate only on performance, not on
personality. Base your evaluation on the typical performance for the entire period not on
isolated instances which are not typical. You should be able to support your rating with
comments and examples that are as specific and as factual as possible.

When you are finished, return the completed form to the Human Resources Department. It
will be sent to your supervisor's immediate supervisor. Your supervisor will <u>not</u> see
your comments.

	Excellent	Good	Fair	Poor
Sets a good example for others	_____	_____	_____	_____
Creates a positive work environment	_____	_____	_____	_____
Motivates employees to do their best	_____	_____	_____	_____
Gives clear directions/communicates well	_____	_____	_____	_____
Is a good listener	_____	_____	_____	_____
Plans and organizes department functions	_____	_____	_____	_____
Is generally fair in decision making	_____	_____	_____	_____
Gives regular feedback on performance	_____	_____	_____	_____
Provides adequate support to complete tasks	_____	_____	_____	_____
Is willing to consider new ideas/suggestions	_____	_____	_____	_____
Is empathetic to employees' concerns	_____	_____	_____	_____
Acts professionally/creates positive image	_____	_____	_____	_____
	_____	_____	_____	_____

Areas of greatest strength:

Areas where improvement is desirable:

General Comments:

_____   _____
Evaluator's Signature (optional)   Date

EMPLOYEE EVALUATION OF SUPERVISOR

Name of Supervisor:_____ Title:_____

Period of Evaluation:_____ to _____

<u>Instructions to the Evaluator</u>: Completion of this form is voluntary - you do not have to evaluate your supervisor if you prefer not to. Your signature at the end is also optional. The purpose is to help supervisors improve their management skills by identifying strengths as well as areas where improvement is desirable.

Do not let your personal feelings affect your rating - rate only on performance, not on personality. Base your evaluation on the typical performance for the entire period not on isolated instances which are not typical. You should be able to support your rating with comments and examples that are as specific and as factual as possible.

When you are finished, return the completed form to the Human Resources Department. It will be sent to your supervisor's immediate supervisor. Your supervisor will <u>not</u> see your comments.

	Excellent	Good	Fair	Poor
Sets a good example for others	_____	_____	_____	_____
Creates a positive work environment	_____	_____	_____	_____
Motivates employees to do their best	_____	_____	_____	_____
Gives clear directions/communicates well	_____	_____	_____	_____
Is a good listener	_____	_____	_____	_____
Plans and organizes department functions	_____	_____	_____	_____
Is generally fair in decision making	_____	_____	_____	_____
Gives regular feedback on performance	_____	_____	_____	_____
Provides adequate support to complete tasks	_____	_____	_____	_____
Is willing to consider new ideas/suggestions	_____	_____	_____	_____
Is empathetic to employees' concerns	_____	_____	_____	_____
Acts professionally/creates positive image	_____	_____	_____	_____

Areas of greatest strength:

Areas where improvement is desirable:

General Comments:

_____ _____   _____
Evaluator's Signature (optional)   Date

EMPLOYEE EVALUATION OF SUPERVISOR

Name of Supervisor:_____ Title:_____
Period of Evaluation:_____ to _____

Instructions to the Evaluator: Completion of this form is voluntary – you do not have to evaluate your supervisor if you prefer not to. Your signature at the end is also optional. The purpose is to help supervisors improve their management skills by identifying strengths as well as areas where improvement is desirable.

Do not let your personal feelings affect your rating – rate only on performance, not on personality. Base your evaluation on the typical performance for the entire period not on isolated instances which are not typical. You should be able to support your rating with comments and examples that are as specific and as factual as possible.

When you are finished, return the completed form to the Human Resources Department. It will be sent to your supervisor's immediate supervisor. Your supervisor will not see your comments.

	Excellent	Good	Fair	Poor
Sets a good example for others	_____	_____	_____	_____
Creates a positive work environment	_____	_____	_____	_____
Motivates employees to do their best	_____	_____	_____	_____
Gives clear directions/communicates well	_____	_____	_____	_____
Is a good listener	_____	_____	_____	_____
Plans and organizes department functions	_____	_____	_____	_____
Is generally fair in decision making	_____	_____	_____	_____
Gives regular feedback on performance	_____	_____	_____	_____
Provides adequate support to complete tasks	_____	_____	_____	_____
Is willing to consider new ideas/suggestions	_____	_____	_____	_____
Is empathetic to employees' concerns	_____	_____	_____	_____
Acts professionally/creates positive image	_____	_____	_____	_____
	_____	_____	_____	_____

Areas of greatest strength:

Areas where improvement is desirable:

General Comments:

_____   _____
Evaluator's Signature (optional)   Date

EMPLOYEE EVALUATION OF SUPERVISOR

Name of Supervisor:_____ Title:_____

Period of Evaluation:_____ to _____

	Excellent	Good	Fair	Poor
Sets a good example for others	_____	_____	_____	_____
Creates a positive work environment	_____	_____	_____	_____
Motivates employees to do their best	_____	_____	_____	_____
Gives clear directions/communicates well	_____	_____	_____	_____
Is a good listener	_____	_____	_____	_____
Plans and organizes department functions	_____	_____	_____	_____
Is generally fair in decision making	_____	_____	_____	_____
Gives regular feedback on performance	_____	_____	_____	_____
Provides adequate support to complete tasks	_____	_____	_____	_____
Is willing to consider new ideas/suggestions	_____	_____	_____	_____
Is empathetic to employees' concerns	_____	_____	_____	_____
Acts professionally/creates positive image	_____	_____	_____	_____

Areas of greatest strength:

Areas where improvement is desirable:

General Comments:

_____   _____
Evaluator's Signature (optional)   Date